BASS FLIES

ILLUSTRATED BY LARRY LARGAY

RICHARD B. STEWART, PUBLISHER
NORTH CONWAY, NEW HAMPSHIRE

DISTRIBUTED BY
NORTHLAND PRESS
BOX 280
INTERVALE, NH 03845

CONTENTS

BASIC TOOLS	4
HOOKS	6
BASS BUG MATERIALS	7
BASIC TYING PROCEDURES	10
DEER HAIR TECHNIQUES	12
WEEDGUARDS	14
NOMENCLATURE	16
BUCKTAILS & STREAMERS	18
CRAYFISH - CRAWDADS	20
DAHLBERG DIVERS	22
DRY FLIES	24
FROGS	26
EELWORM STREAMERS	28
GRASSHOPPERS	29
HAIRBUGS	30
JIGS	32
LEECHES	33
MATCH-THE-MINNOW	34
MOTHS	35
MOUSE RAT	36
MUDDLERS	37
NYMPHS	38
POPPERS	40
SCULPINS & BULLHEADS	42
SHAD	44
WOOLLY BUGGERS	45
ZONKERS	46
BIBLIOGRAPHY	47
INDEX	48

OTHER BOOKS BY DICK STEWART:
    UNIVERSAL FLY TYING GUIDE
    TROLLING FLIES FOR TROUT AND SALMON (WITH BOB LEEMAN)
    THE HOOK BOOK

ISBN 0-936644-03-6 HARDCOVER
ISBN 0-936644-04-4 SOFTCOVER

INTRODUCTION

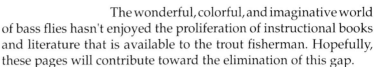

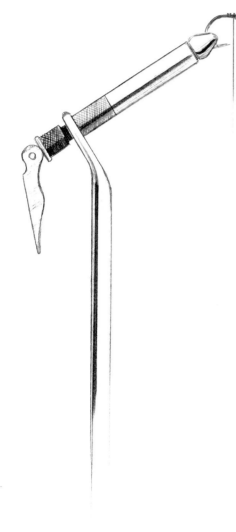

The wonderful, colorful, and imaginative world of bass flies hasn't enjoyed the proliferation of instructional books and literature that is available to the trout fisherman. Hopefully, these pages will contribute toward the elimination of this gap.

It was some 30 plus years ago that I was first introduced to fly tying by a kindly, gray-haired gentleman whose name I have unfortunately let lapse in my memory, but whose first love was tying bass bugs for smallmouth bass fishing along the Delaware River. From these beginnings, with a lap full of deer body hair trimmings, many scraggly, yet successful, bass and panfish flies evolved; this was followed in turn by a more diversified fly tying practice with trout and salmon flies of every description.

Since those days the world of fly tying has been revolutionized with the advent of new techniques, materials, and knowledge. Although many bass flies maintain their similarity to the traditional versions, the newer patterns do, indeed, present many significant improvements. It seems certain that with the rapidly growing interest in fly rodding for bass, it will only be a short time before more information will be uncovered, and this added knowledge will lead toward the further evolution of fly patterns.

Many people have unknowingly contributed to this book, and throughout these pages I have attempted to identify some of these fly tyers with their creations. Often, however, fly patterns are less the product of invention and more the result of evolution as skilled tyers recognize valuable new ideas from multiple sources, and then include them in their own efforts. In these instances the originator of a design or technique might not be recognized, as their idea is borrowed and incorporated into another's pattern. My purpose is to fully share knowledge about bass flies and I would like to thank all of those unnamed contributors.

But most importantly, it is to the anonymous gray-haired instructor of my youth that I should like to dedicate this book.

Basic Tools

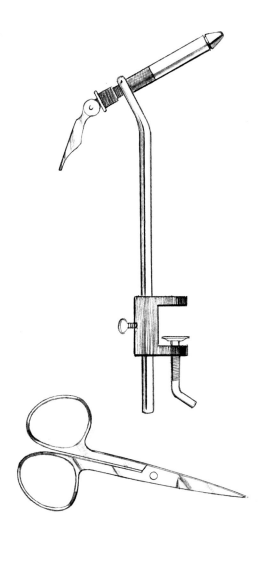

VISE — The most important, and usually the most expensive tool used in fly tying is the vise. Its primary function is to hold the hook securely, and this is particularly important in the construction of bass flies due to the increased thread tension often employed in the tying of these larger flies. The basic vise is called a stationary vise because it generally remains in one position, although it may have several possible adjustments for height or angle. A second type, called a rotary vise, can be used either as a stationary model, or may be rotated to assist in the winding of materials. Features to look for in a vise include the ability to securely hold a wide range of hook sizes, smoothness of the finish, height adjustments, ease of operation, and the means of securing it to a desk or table.

SCISSORS — Small, very sharp scissors with narrow fine points are indispensable for the detailed work of fly tying. Large finger holes are preferred by experienced tyers who like to keep the scissors on their fingers throughout the tying procedure. In the tying of bass flies it is particularly important to also have a heavy duty scissor to be used in the cutting of coarse materials like deer body hair. This hair will quickly ruin a fine tipped scissor. For bass fly construction I prefer my heavy duty scissors to be curved, with a serrated and/or self-sharpening blade.

BOBBIN — This is a tool which holds the spool of thread during the tying operation. The bobbin permits very accurate control of the placement of each individual thread winding on the hook, and also helps you to control the thread tension which is so important in the building of a strong, durable fly. The bobbin also provides sufficient weight to prevent unravelling of thread when the hands must be free for other purposes. Of particular interest to the bass fly tyer are the new ceramic bobbins, or more precisely, bobbins with a hard ceramic tube that won't wear down to a sharp edge the way so many metal bobbins do.

BODKIN — A simple, inexpensive device consisting of a needle inserted into a handle for the sake of convenience. It is used for a variety of tasks such as applying head cement, picking out stray fibers, cleaning out the eye of a hook, separating fibers, and picking out dubbing fur. Some bodkins feature a half hitch tool as their handle, others incorporate a built in magnet with which to pick up hooks. Hopefully some supplier will combine a bodkin with a hair packing tool for the bass bug tyer.

HAIR PACKER — This tool is used to push spun deer body hair toward the rear of the hook, packing it tightly together to achieve a neat, compact body. A similarly functioning device can be made using the external barrel of a ball point pen.

HACKLE PLIERS — These are used to grip hackle feathers by the tips and to hold them securely as they are wound around or applied to the fly. They must have a firm grip as hackles have a tendency to slip out of the jaws quite easily. Sharp edges on the pliers can cut the feather and should be avoided.

BOBBIN THREADER — A device used to draw the tying thread through the small tube of your bobbin. Very inexpensive yet saves on patience when needed.

RAZOR BLADES — Single edged razor blades are commonly used to cut and shape spun deer body hair when tying any of the hair bugs so commonly used for bass.

HALF HITCH TOOL — This is used to make simple half hitch knots at the head of a fly.

HAIR STACKER — Consists of a tube into which bucktail or other hair is inserted, tips downward, then tapped against a desk or table, to evenly align the hair tips when used for wings or tails.

WHIP FINISHER — A tool which requires practice to use properly, but once mastered enables one to rapidly tie a whip finish knot, the most secure manner to tie off your thread upon completion of a fly.

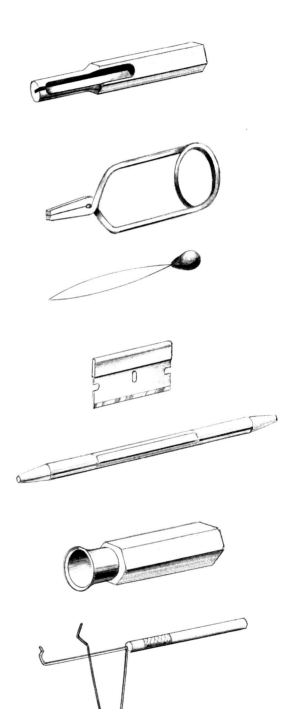

HOOKS

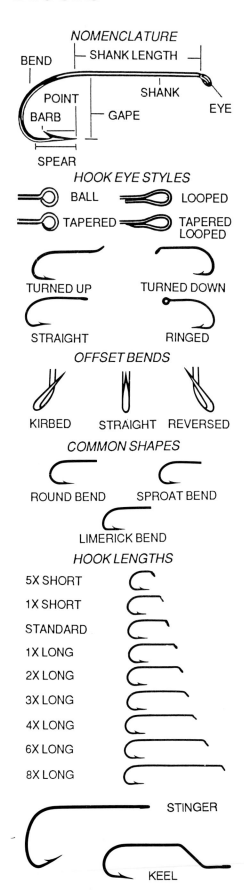

NOMENCLATURE

BEND — SHANK LENGTH —
SHANK
POINT
BARB — GAPE —
EYE
SPEAR

HOOK EYE STYLES

BALL   LOOPED
TAPERED   TAPERED LOOPED

TURNED UP   TURNED DOWN
STRAIGHT   RINGED

OFFSET BENDS

KIRBED   STRAIGHT   REVERSED

COMMON SHAPES

ROUND BEND   SPROAT BEND
LIMERICK BEND

HOOK LENGTHS

5X SHORT
1X SHORT
STANDARD
1X LONG
2X LONG
3X LONG
4X LONG
6X LONG
8X LONG

STINGER
KEEL

Dave Whitlock once aptly described the hook as the "backbone of a fly", meaning that the rigid hook dictates the shape, form, weight, and sometimes even the action of the fly which is tied on it. Fly tyers should always be aware of this and should not assume that all hooks are similar.

For the bass fisherman the range of hooks needed is not as large as that required by the trout fisherman, particularly in the smaller sizes. Some basic wet fly type hooks, some 2X to 4X long streamer type hooks, a few larger dry fly hooks, and something on which to tie the deer hair bugs(such as a stinger-type hook) will certainly get you started. For largemouth bass the size range should probably be from size 1/0 to 6, whereas flies for smallmouth bass will most commonly be tied on hooks which range from size 2 to size 10.

The majority of hooks available to fly tyers have a bronze finish, meaning that they have been coated with a bronze colored lacquer. Some tyers have been increasingly experimenting with stainless steel hooks, or else those which are silver or gold coated. A few hooks are blued and a few have been "Japanned", meaning they have been coated with a black lacquer.

All hooks should be sharpened before tying your bass flies. Except for some of the new chemically sharpened hooks, you will find that most commercial hooks simply don't have the sharpest possible point as they are received from the manufacturer. It's worth your while to take a file or sharpening stone and to touch up the points before proceeding to tie your fly. This practice may well help increase your percentage of hook-ups while fishing.

The accompanying chart shows you the common terms used in reference to your fly tying hooks. Also pictured is a chart showing the relative lengths of hook shanks using the terminology most often used by the manufacturers.

With the increading interest in flyfishing for bass, we will most likely see the introducion of a greater variety of hooks specifically designed with the bass fisherman in mind. Bass fishermen need hooks with a strength that will permit them to "cross the eyes" of bass when setting the hooks. This additional strength is particularly important when you need to apply extra pressure, having hooked your quarry in some heavy weeds or brush. I anticipate that over the next few years some hook manufacturers will offer new specialty models designed for the bass fisherman.

The materials described here represent those most commonly used in tying bass flies. Many are available through a great variety of sources, others must be purchased through more specialized fly tying materials suppliers. While these are the traditional and tested materials, one should not hesitate to experiment with other materials for this is how we progress. The field of tying bass flies is not tradition bound, so if you don't have some of the materials required, substitution is quite acceptable for personal flies; however, be certain the replacement material has characteristics similar to the original specified material.

THREAD - Fly tying thread is made of twisted silk or nylon. The latter is most available, and generally stronger, but does stretch slightly. Thread diameter is usually designated by numbers beginning with 1/0 through the smaller 8/0. Even larger threads progress from size "A" through the larger size "E". Small threads build up less bulk and weight than large threads, but are not as strong. Untwisted flat nylon threads are now commonly available in three sizes, which seem to satisfy the requirements of most fly tyers. The first type, called Mono Cord, is available waxed or unwaxed and is good for most types of bass flies where strength is required. The smaller type is generally described as fine PreWaxed Nylon and sold under various brand names. It's recommended for all smaller flies, especially drys. The heaviest of the flat threads is actually a flat waxed floss, ideal where maximum strength is needed. Recently a thread made of Kevlar has reached the market which, while considerably stronger than conventional materials, is yet in the experimental stages as far as many fly tyers are concerned.

BODY MATERIALS - Are those materials produced in a form which is simply wrapped on the hook shank to create the fly body. Tinsel is a flat metallic colored tape, usually gold or silver, and most commonly available in fine, medium, and wide sizes. Originally constructed of thin metal, a mylar plastic tinsel is now frequently used because it doesn't have sharp edges and doesn't tarnish. Also it can be woven into a tubular form to form a tinsel braid, and more recently it's been made into a chenille as well. Oval tinsel in similar colors and sizes is also frequently specified for bodies and ribbing. Wool of all sorts is used, especially on wet flies and streamers since it tends to absorb water and sinks well. Orlon, Acrylic, or Polypropylene yarns are all good and seem to float better. Floss is made of silk, nylon, or acetate and is used mostly for sinking flies. It is readily available in a wide variety of colors. Spun fur is usually rabbit fur made into a yarn in various dyed colors. It's easy to work with and

has a fuzzy appearance desirable on many flies. Chenille of nylon or rayon is sold in many sizes and colors and is best for sinking flies. Latex comes in sheet form which can be cut into strips and dyed or marked various colors. It sinks rapidly and is effective on many nymph patterns.

FEATHERS - This broad category is widely used in fly tying and probably every imaginable type of feather has been tried at one time or another. Hackle refers to feathers from the neck of a bird, most commonly a rooster. For dry flies a long, glossy, stiff hackle is desirable whereas for wet flies a soft, dull hackle is appropriate. Hackles from grouse or partridge or other birds are often short and soft and referred to as "soft hackles". Extra long, thin hackles from the rump of a rooster are called saddle hackles and are used for streamer flies, larger drys, and are of particular importance for many of the bass fly patterns such as Eelworm Streamers or wound hackles on Woolly Buggers. Quills generally refer to the primary or secondary wing quills of any bird. Goose, duck, and turkey quills in either natural or dyed colors are commonly used for tails and wings on a variety of flies. Tail feathers of some birds are used, mostly turkey and ringneck pheasant. The Crest is the topmost feathers on the head of the bird. Golden pheasant crest feathers are frequently specified in fly patterns Tippets refer to the barred feathers from the lower neck of golden and amherst pheasants. Herl is part of a peacock or ostrich plume which has a long flexible stem and very short barbules. Peacock herl with its metallic sheen is an important fly tying ingredient. Maribou was originally a soft stork feather but now refers to the long downy under-feather from turkeys. It's often a replacement for streamer wings due to its undulating motion in water. Flank feathers from the sides of woodduck, teal, pintail, and mallard ducks are one of the most popular fly wing materials. Body feathers of all descriptions are used from time to time and may be referred to as back feathers, breast feathers, or rump feathers. Best known to fly tyers are those from silver and ringneck pheasants, as well as various ducks.

TAILS - An assortment of animal tails provides the fly tyer with an inexpensive supply of materials that have the qualities of length and/or stiffness. Bucktails, usually from the whitetail deer species provide a readily dyed source of hair used for the "Bucktail" flies, for dry fly wings and other purposes. It's best to avoid the extremely crinkled hair. Calftails have a finer and more translucent hair used frequently for dry fly wings and often substituted for bucktail. Again, avoid hair that is extremely crinkled and curled. Squirrel tails of either the grey or red species have a fine straight hair and are also

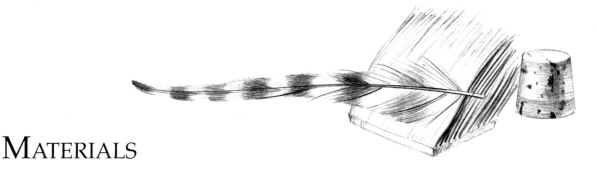

MATERIALS

used in dyed colors. Minktails, in a range of natural and dyed colors have increased in popularity as their stiff hairs have proved excellent for dry fly tails and caddis fly wings. Woodchuck tails are used in the same manner as minktails.

HAIR - This category refers to the stiffer hairs, from the bodies of various animals. Most body hair of some animals, specifically deer, antelope, caribou, elk and moose, is stiff and generally hollow. It's used in various ways for tails, wings, and spun bodies and heads on many flies and such hair is of particular value to the tyer of bass bugs. It is important to become familiar with the properties of the various hairs so that you can utilize the unique characteristics of each to achieve the desired results. Each species, indeed each skin will have hair that's soft or stiff, short or long, coarse or fine; practice with spinning or stacking each type will soon teach you how to select hair to achieve specific ends. Guard hairs (i.e. long stiffer hair as distinguished from short soft underfur) of various animals such as badger, grey fox, and woodchuck are occasionally used for streamer or salmon fly wings.

FURS - Mostly used as a dubbing material to form bodies, furs of all types and descriptions are a basic material for fly tyers. Various colors can be mixed and blended to provide any color tone desired. Unprocessed furs, particularly from water-dwelling animals such as muskrat, otter, and beaver, contain natural oils which make them resistant to water absorption. Furs when washed, bleached, or dyed lose this quality. Very fine furs such as rabbit are easiest to work with and available in many natural and dyed colors. A medium textured fur would be Australian possum which combines general ease of use plus a rougher texture to often give buggy effect. Seal fur is a very coarse and somewhat difficult fur to use properly; it, and its substitutes, have a sheen and translucency which makes for a brighter fly. Fur from a European hare's mask goes into the popular Hare's Ear dry fly, wet fly, and nymph.

SYNTHETICS - The non-availability or expense of many materials, combined with the growing variety of nylon, acrylic, rayon, dynel, kodel, mylar, and polypropylene, and many other synthetics has led to substitutes, experimentation, and frequently improvement. Leading the list of synthetics today must be the variety of synthetic furs on the market. These are being offered in various textures and colors selected especially for fly tyers. One must match the particular synthetic to its intended use to obtain the desired qualities. Polypropylene (Poly) as a dubbing fur is lighter than water but this advantage is offset by hook weight unless the fly has the additional

support of a tail and hackle. Synthetics like this do not, however, become waterlogged and dry off when casting. Conversely, when synthetics are used on heavier wet fly hooks they tend to sink faster than natural furs. Imitation seal fur, imitation polar bear, and imitation bucktail have all proved their usefulness. Synthetic yarns, while already accepted in many forms, are finding increased usage as technology advances. Sparkle yarn comes to us via DuPont and offers the fly tyer more light reflection. Poly yarn has been utilized for dry fly wings. Imitation jungle cock replaces the natural feather from the jungle fowl, a bird on the Endangered Species list. Nylon raffia is a straw-like material which can be used for dry fly wings or the wing cases on nymphs. Recently a whole new generation of sparkly, bright or prismatic materials has been introduced which have had great acceptance from bass fly tyers. Sold under names such as Flashabou, Krystal Hair, Crystal Flash and such, these are now commonly available in a wide range of colors. The list could go on extensively but many synthetics are still experimental, while others will certainly come forth in the future.

OTHER MATERIALS - In order to add weight to flies lead wire in various sizes is tied onto, or wrapped around the hook shank. New, dumbbell shaped lead eyes, or beadchain, serve both as eyes and weight the fly as well. Various plastic eyes are available for the fly tyer through supply houses. To help secure portions of the fly and make it more durable, a flexible cement such as Dave's Fleximent, Vinyl Cement or others is useful. It can also be applied to wing quill segments to prevent splitting. Head Cement or lacquer, either clear or colored, is essential to coat the thread windings at the head of a fly upon completion to prevent loosening, and is also used for painted eyes. To paint cork, balsa, or lead jigs, some of the new acrylic paints have proved effective. Dubbing wax of a semi-tacky consistency is used when making fur dubbed bodies. Waterproof markers in a range of colors permit instant dying of some materials or the addition of realistic markings on some flies. In the final analysis, the possibilities are myriad for the hobbiest, and it's up to you to experiment with a wide variety of materials to achieve your desired results.

GLOSSARY

Antron - a bright, triangular fibered, synthetic wool

Badger - a hackle with a black center stripe

Barb - part of a hook, see page 6

Bend - see description of hooks, page 6

Beard - a method of applying throat hackle on underside of hook

Bobbin - tool used to hold tying thread, see page 4

Bodkin - a needle-like tool with handle, see page 4

Braided Tinsel - Mylar braided over a cotton core

Bucktail - hair from tail of a deer; also a style of fly which uses bucktail as its principal material

Bullhead - a common, bottom dwelling, baitfish

Caddis Fly - Type of common aquatic insect

Cement - an adhesive used in fly tying

Chamois - a suede-like, flexible, thin leather

Collar - hair or hackle, wound as a throat

Cree - a hackle of mixed white, brown, and gray markings

Crystal Flash - a highly reflective, sparkly, synthetic hair

Crystal Hair - see Crystal Flash

Dry Fly - an artificial fly which floats upon water surface

Dubbing - a technique of applying fur; also refers to the fur itself

Dumbbell Eyes - small lead eyes, moulded into the shape of dumbbells or barbells

Eye - part of a hook, see page 6

Fishair - a synthetic similar to bucktail

Flank - the side of a bird or duck

Flashabou - a limp plastic tinsel available in many colors

Furnace - a brown hackle with a black center stripe

Fur Strip - narrow strips of skin, with fur intact, usually of rabbit

Furry Foam - a sheet foam material with a velvet-like surface on each side

Gape - part of a hook measurement, see page 6

Grizzly - black and white barred hackle from a Barred Rock or Plymouth Rock chicken

Hackle - feather from the neck or back of a bird, most frequently from a rooster neck unless otherwise noted

Hackle Pliers - a tool used to grip hackle, see page 5

Hair Compacter - a tool used to compress spun deer body hair. See page 5

Halfhitch - the simplest knot used to secure thread

Hen - a female chicken, pheasant or duck

Keel Hook - a hook style designed to be weedless

Lacquer - a head cement, usually offered in colors

Larva - first immature stage of insects having a complete life cycle

Matuka - a style of streamer fly, see page 19

Monocord - a flat, untwisted nylon thread

Monofilament - single strand, clear nylon fishing line

Mylar - flat metallic colored plastic ribbon or tape, used as a nontarnishing tinsel

Neck - the complete skin with hackle feathers from a chicken, most often a rooster

Nymph - immature aquatic first stage of insects. Longevity from 1 to 3 years

Orlon - a synthetic yarn, tends not to absorb water

Oval Tinsel - a tinsel wrapped around a cotton thread

Palmer - hackle wrapped over the body of a fly

Polypropylene - a synthetic material, lighter than water

Prewaxed - thread waxed at factory

Prismatic Tape - a highly reflective metallic, adhesive backed tape

Quill - commonly refers to feathers from the wing of a bird; also the stem of any feather

Rubber Hackle - narrow rubber band-like ribbons of rubber

Saddle - the rear back portion of a chicken

Salmon Hook - a style of black lacquered hook with a turned-up loop eye

Sculpin - a common bottom dwelling bait fish

Shank - part of a hook, see page 6

Soft Hackle - a short, soft, webby hackle for wet flies, usually hen, partridge, or grouse hackle

Sparkle Yarn - synthetic yarn containing Antron

Sparse - indicates materials applied very sparingly

Spinning - a method of using deer body hair, see page 12

Split Bead - hollow metal bead, split open on one side

Stacking - a method of using deer body hair, see page 14

Stem - the center supporting quill of any feather

Streamer - type of fly designed to imitate small fish, usually made of feathers

Stripped - feather from which the individual barbs have been removed

Swiss Straw - a flat grass-like synthetic nylon

Tinsel - metal or metallic plastic ribbon-like material

Underhair - the softer hair near the skin

Web - the soft, dull, webby lower center portion of a hackle

Weighted - a fly with lead wire wrapped or tied on the shank

Wet Fly - a traditional style of fly that sinks in water

Whip Finish - the best knot with which to finish flies

BASIC TYING PROCEDURES - BUCKTAILS

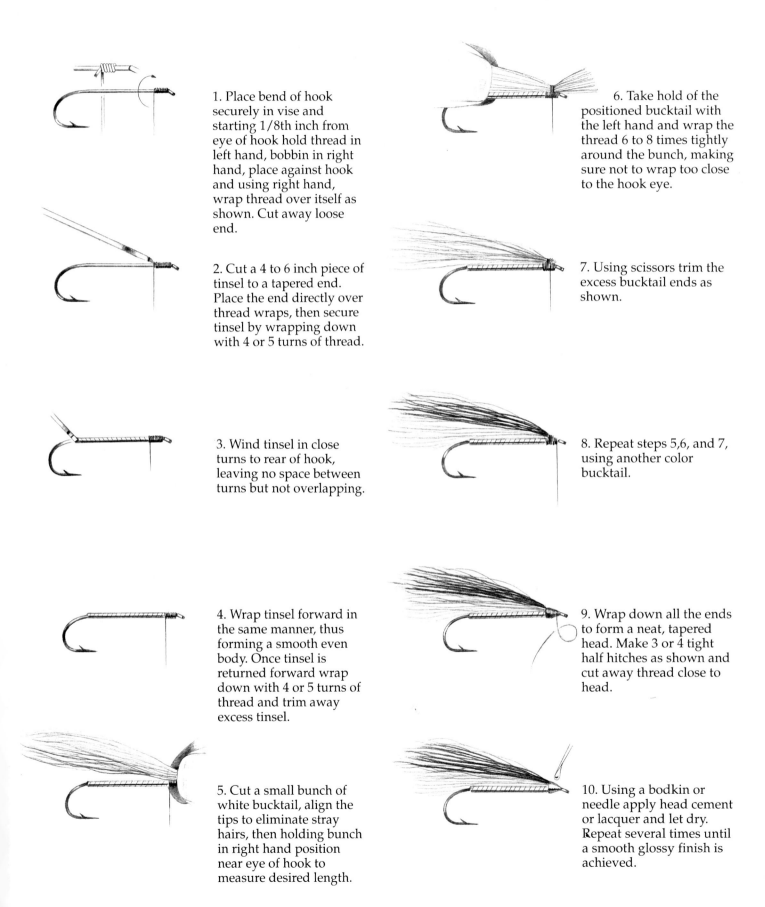

1. Place bend of hook securely in vise and starting 1/8th inch from eye of hook hold thread in left hand, bobbin in right hand, place against hook and using right hand, wrap thread over itself as shown. Cut away loose end.

2. Cut a 4 to 6 inch piece of tinsel to a tapered end. Place the end directly over thread wraps, then secure tinsel by wrapping down with 4 or 5 turns of thread.

3. Wind tinsel in close turns to rear of hook, leaving no space between turns but not overlapping.

4. Wrap tinsel forward in the same manner, thus forming a smooth even body. Once tinsel is returned forward wrap down with 4 or 5 turns of thread and trim away excess tinsel.

5. Cut a small bunch of white bucktail, align the tips to eliminate stray hairs, then holding bunch in right hand position near eye of hook to measure desired length.

6. Take hold of the positioned bucktail with the left hand and wrap the thread 6 to 8 times tightly around the bunch, making sure not to wrap too close to the hook eye.

7. Using scissors trim the excess bucktail ends as shown.

8. Repeat steps 5,6, and 7, using another color bucktail.

9. Wrap down all the ends to form a neat, tapered head. Make 3 or 4 tight half hitches as shown and cut away thread close to head.

10. Using a bodkin or needle apply head cement or lacquer and let dry. Repeat several times until a smooth glossy finish is achieved.

10

BASIC TYING PROCEDURES - DRY FLIES

1. Begin by forming a thread base at the point of wing attachment.

2. Tie in a bunch of bucktail, tips even and forward, and trim away excess butt ends to a taper. Wrap tightly to secure in place.

3. Pull wing upright and make several thread turns immediately in front to hold wing up.

4. Divide wing into 2 equal bunches and criss-cross thread through the middle.

5. Select 2 rooster hackles; strip away the lower soft barbules, and attach as shown.

6. Move thread to rear and attach a bucktail tail as shown.

7. Apply body material or dubbing to form body.

8. Pull hackles upright, then wrap first hackle mostly behind wing and tie down tip.

9. Wrap second hackle, mostly in front of wing, and tie down tip.

10. Closely cut away tips, form head with very few turns of thread, and whip finish.

Spinning Deer Body Hair

The following instructions are intended to provide explicit directions in the technique of spinning deer body hair for use in bass bugs, or any fly using deer body hair. All drawings are from the perspective of a right handed fly tyer and left handed persons will have to make the proper adjustments.

1. Select a hook of your choice (beginners should start with a size 2,4 or 6 hook) and place in the vise. Note the position of the point. Although this point may seem to interfere with your thread wraps, you will soon learn to avoid it. If you were to bury the point within the vise jaws you run a risk of weakening the hook itself.

2. Fasten your tying thread to the hook shank as shown. Only a few wraps are needed to provide an achor point. Size "A" nylon thread is recommended because it has the needed strength and its diameter is large enough to minumize its cutting into the deer body hair as you draw it tight.

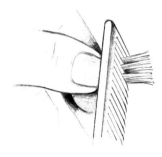

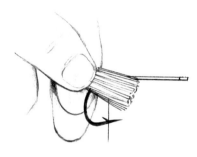

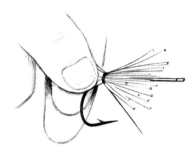

6. Hold the deer hair bunch by the tips and again using a comb or wire brush, completely remove the fuzzy underhair.

7. Holding the bunch of deer body hair in your left hand, and controlling your thread with the right hand, lay the hair directly over the thread anchor point. It should be placed at an angle of about 45 degrees to the top of the hook shank. Your right hand should be lightly holding the thread below the hook.

8. Continuing to hold the deer body hair in position with your left hand, make 2 winds around the hair and hook shank. The amount of thread tension used at this stage is very important. The first wind should barely nestle against the hair, the second wind, directly over the first, should begin to compress the hair. Throughout these wraps maintain the position of the hair with the left hand.

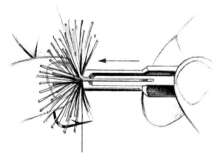

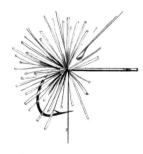

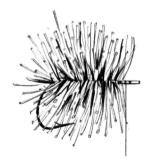

12. Before proceeding to the next bunch, you should compress the first one. Using your left hand, firmly grasp the hook shank directly behind the hair. Using a hair compacting tool in your right hand, or your fingers, firmly push against the hair, sliding it toward the rear.

13. At this point it's a good idea to make a half-hitch of thread immediately in front of the hair. This reduces the chance of any loosening as you proceed. Also, a drop or two of cement placed on the thread winds, and spreading into the hair, will add to the fly's durability.

14. Repeat Steps 3 to 13 as many times as needed to complete a body of the desired length. When finished make an additional 2 or 3 half hitches in front to firmly secure the thread.

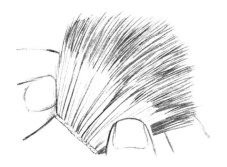

3. Select a piece of clean deer body hair with individual hairs at least 1 inch in length. If the hair is very long (over 2 inches), by careful planning you can often get two bunches from each length. You don't want the hair to be excessively long as any substantial excess simply gets in the way.

4. Using a comb or wire brush, remove any foreign matter by stroking the hair along the "grain."

5. Select a small clump of the deer body hair and cut off with your scissors. The size of the clump will depend on many factors such as the size and type of fly you're building, the texture of the piece of deer hair, and your skill and experience with this technique. The most usual size bunch will have a diameter about the size of an ordinary wood lead pencil.

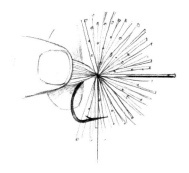

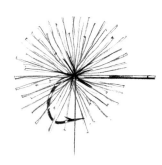

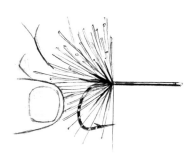

9. The next wraps will spin the hair around the hook shank. Your third wrap is to be made under increased, but not full, tension. As you make this turn of thread gradually loosen your grasp of the deer body hair. As you do so the hair will begin to flare, and will also start to "spin" around the hook shank following the direction of your thread turns.

10. Fully release control with the left hand and continue spinning the deer body hair by making another 3 to 6 thread turns (depending on the size of your original bunch of hair). All thread wraps shoud be made directly atop of one another.

11. Having completed the spinning of the deer body hair, move your left hand to a position in front of the hair. Gently fold the hair toward the rear so as to clear a space for you to attach the next bunch of hair. As you do this with the left hand, take control of the thread with the right hand. Making one wrap through the spun hair, advance the thread forward to the bare hook shank directly in front.

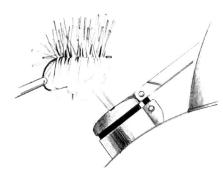

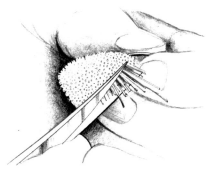

15. Cut the thread and remove the hook from the vise in preparation for trimming and shaping the hair. If you are seeking exacting results you might try steaming the spun hair over a tea kettle.

16. On most flies it is best to begin by cutting the hair flat on the underside. This is best accomplished with a sharp single edge razor blade, however, scissors may be used or even electric hair clippers. This close, flat trimming is needed to clear the gape by removing any bulk that might interfere with the finished fly's hooking ability.

17. Once the bottom is flattened the remaining parts may be shaped as desired. Proceed cautiously on your first efforts—you can always remove more later.

STACKING

Stacking is a technique for using deer body hair, or similar material, for the specific and exact placement of bunches of hair. The method allows the use of a broader range of hair stiffness than may be used in spinning, and you may wish to experiment with various textures for different of results. The outcome of this technique is the ability to layer colors on your fly. An example might be a hair frog with a green back and a creamy yellow belly.

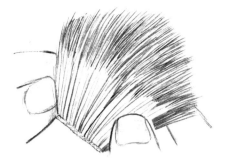

1. Select a bunch of deer body hair and prepare it in the same manner as though you were going to be spinning the hair.

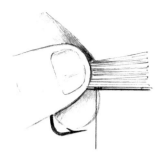

2. Gripping the hair tightly with the left hand, and holding it parallel to the hook shank at the point of desired attachment, begin by making a soft loop of thread over the hair.

STACKING COLORS

Stacking colors is a method of stacking 2 or even 3 colors, each one directly on top of the preceding color. The technique is that of stacking. What differs is the placement of the succeeding bunches of hair to achieve the desired effect. The result will be like the spots on a frog, a color within a color, within a color. This is not the easiest of techniques to execute, so don't worry if your first efforts don't turn out right.

1. Begin by spinning two bunches of deer body hair and then bringing your tying thread to the center of the bunch.

2. Select another bunch of a different colored deer body hair and, holding it parallel to the hook shank, stack it centered directly on top of the spun deer hair.

WEEDGUARDS

Some bass fishermen argue that all bass flies should have weed guards—others believe in the use of weed guards only when absolutely necessary. Over the years at least a dozen different styles of weed guards have been used but we have limited ourselves to the basic, now-standard, monofilament weed guard which has proved to be so successful.

1. Begin by winding a long base of tight thread winds along the hook shank as shown.

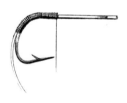

2. Firmly attach a length of monofilament which is just a bit smaller in size than the diameter of the hook shank. Tie off. Now you are ready to proceed to tie your fly.

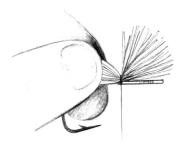

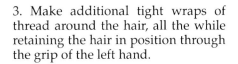

3. Make additional tight wraps of thread around the hair, all the while retaining the hair in position through the grip of the left hand.

4. Still controlling the hair with the left hand make 2 or 3 final, very tight turns. Release the left hand grip and gently pull all the hair upward and together. At this point you may wish to further tighten up the hair by making a wrap or two aroung the base of the clump.

`5. Repeat this process with a different color hair, only this time place the hair directly below the first bunch, on the bottom. Be certain to keep this hair separate from the first bunch, and when trimmed you'll have a two-tone result.

3. Repeat step 2 using yet another color of deer body hair. You should now have 3 layers of stacked deer body hair, each a different color.

4. Move your thread forward and now spin on one more bunch of your original color of deer body hair, in front of the prior batches.

5. When trimmed, the hair should look like this, with a spot of color within which is contained your second color.

3. Once your fly is complete, and your tying thread is moved to a position just behind the eye of the hook, bring the monofilament forward and through the eye of the hook.

4. Adjust the monofilament so that the loop portion extends just about 1/4 inch to 3/16 inch below the hook point.

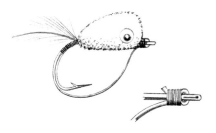

5. Using your tying thread, secure the monofilament by wrapping it down behind the hook eye. Cut away excess, and tie off.

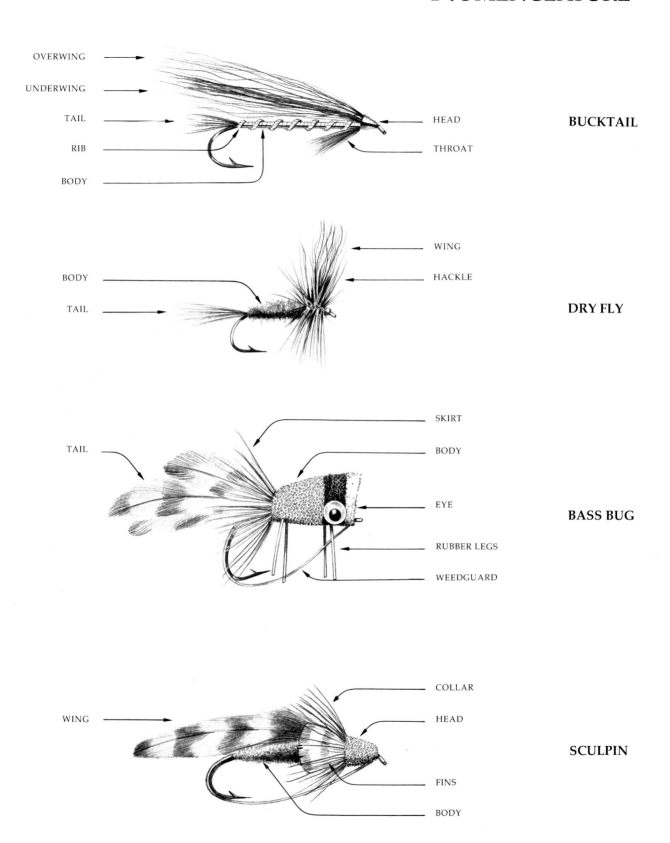

OVERWING

UNDERWING

TAIL

RIB

BODY

HEAD

THROAT

BUCKTAIL

BODY

TAIL

WING

HACKLE

DRY FLY

TAIL

SKIRT

BODY

EYE

RUBBER LEGS

WEEDGUARD

BASS BUG

WING

COLLAR

HEAD

FINS

BODY

SCULPIN

BUCKTAILS &

MICKEY FINN

CLAUSER'S BABY SMALLMOUTH

CARDINELLE

SHENK'S WHITE STREAMER

Mickey Finn
Thread: Black, **Body**: Flat silver tinsel, **Rib**: Oval silver tinsel, **Wing**: Yellow bucktail, over red bucktail, over yellow bucktail. One of the bread-and-butter bucktails well known to fly fishermen everywhere.

Clauser's Baby Smallmouth (Bob Clauser)
Thread: Olive, **Eyes**: Lead dumbbell shape, tied on top of shank, red with black pupil, **Wing**: Bucktail - Dk. brown over dk. olive over 6 strands of gold Crystal Flash mixed with brown Flashabou, over dk. green over white. On a 1X long hook, and without a body, the lead eyes bounce this one on the bottom.

Cardinelle (Paul Kukonen)
Thread: Fluorescent red, **Body**: Fluorescent red wool **Wing**: Fluorescent red fishair, over which is cerise marabou, **Throat**: Yellow hackle collar. A great fly for just about every gamefish species.

Shenk's White Streamer (Ed Shenk)
Thread; White, **Tail**: White marabou, **Body**: White rabbit fur spun on as a body using the loop dubbing technique, and clipped to shape. This style, in all black or all white, provides bass flyrodders with a simple fly which can be fished with confidence.

1. Attach thread, tie on oval tinsel securing along full length of body, move thread forward and attach flat silver tinsel.

2. Wrap flat tinsel to rear and return it over itself finishing at the front. Spiral the oval tinsel ribbing to the front.

3. Select a small bunch of yellow bucktail and place on top of the hook, tie down tightly with 5 or 6 turns of thread.

4. Using an equal size bunch of red bucktail, place on top of the first bunch. Again, tie down tightly.

5. Select a larger bunch of yellow bucktail to go on top of the red. Tie down tightly, cement, trim and tie off with half hitches or a whip finish.

1. Attach thread, then attach and wrap a full length wool body.

2. Cut a small bunch of fluorescent red/orange Fishair and secure on top, extending to just beyond the hook bend.

3. Add cerise marabou directly on top of the Fishair. Trim away excess.

4. Select a yellow hackle of medium stiffness and tie in as illustrated.

5. Wind the hackle forming a collar. Tie off, and make a few winds to make the hackle point backward. Form head and whip finish.

18

STREAMERS

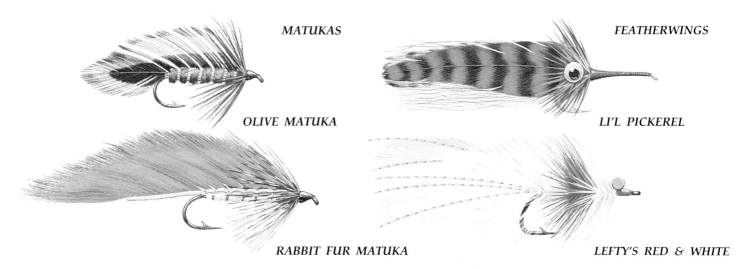

MATUKAS

OLIVE MATUKA

RABBIT FUR MATUKA

FEATHERWINGS

LI'L PICKEREL

LEFTY'S RED & WHITE

Olive Matuka
Thread: Black, **Body**: Olive chenille, with red wool at the gills, **Rib**: Fine oval gold tinsel, **Wing**: Badger hackles dyed olive, **Throat**: Same as wing. The matuka style, originating in New Zealand, provides for binding down the wing with the ribbing material, thus preventing its twisting under the hook.

Rabbit Fur Matuka
Thread: Black, **Body**: White wool with red at the gills, **Rib**: Fine oval silver tinsel, **Wing**: Gray rabbit fur strip, **Throat**: Grizzly hen hackle. The soft fur strip wing adds motion to the fly.

Lefty's Red & White (Lefty Kreh)
Thread: Red, **Tail**: 6 white neck hackles, splayed outward, with 3 strands of pearl Crystal Hair on each side, **Body**: 40% white hackle, then 40% red hackle, then 20% white hackle. Lefty considers this the "single most effective underwater fly that I have ever used for bass."

Li'l Pickerel (Dick Stewart)
Thread: Olive, **Tail**: Olive bucktail flanked by 6 grizzly saddle hackles dyed olive, plus a short bunch of olive marabou, **Eyes**: Doll eyes to keep the fly bouyant, **Collar**: Soft grizzly dyed olive

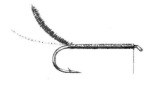

1. Attach thread, tie on oval tinsel (or wire) for rib, and attach chenille body material.

2. Wrap body to the front and add one or two turns of red wool as gills.

3. Attach 2 or 4 hackles as shown. These should be placed with concave sides together.

4. Stroke the hackle fibers upright and spiral the tinsel rib forward, thus securing the hackles.

5. Attach a hackle at the head, and wrap 3 or 4 turns to form a collar. Another few turns will point the collar rearward. Trim, tie off and cement.

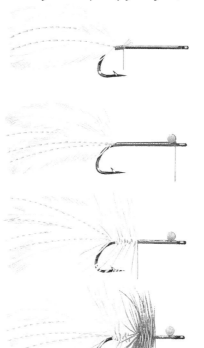

1. Tie on 6 white neck hackles, 3 on each side, convex sides together, and splayed outward. Add 3 strands of Crystal Hair on each side.

2. Tie on a pair of lead dumbbell eyes at the front.

3. At the rear tie in one large white soft rooster hackle and wrap forward to cover the rear 40 percent of the shank.

4. Add a large soft rooster hackle, dyed red, and wrap forward covering the next 40 percent of hook shank.

5. Finish by winding on another white hackle over the remaining 20 percent of the hook shank. Tie off and cement.

crayfish crawdads

CLAUSER'S CRAYFISH
(Bob Clouser)

Hook:	3X long, sizes 4 to 8
Thread:	Tan or beige monocord
Weight:	Square lead wire on each side of shank
Antennae:	6 cock pheasant tail fibers
Nose:	Tip of hen mallard flank
Claws:	Hen mallard flank cut into a V shape
Body:	Very pale green sparkle yarn dubbing
Legs:	Bleached grizzly hackle
Back & Head:	Tan, olive, or brown Furry Foam

CRAWDAD CREEPER
(Rick Hafele)

Hook:	3X or 4X long, sizes 6 and 8
Thread:	Olive
Pincers:	Red squirrel tail
Legs:	Long, light tan, soft hackle
Body:	Olive yarn or dubbing
Shellback & Tail:	Red squirrel tail

CRAWDAD SHEDDER
(Ed Howey)

Hook:	4X long, sizes 2 to 12
Thread:	Tan or brown
Claws:	Deer body hair
Underbody:	Weighted - lead wire; unweighted - wool yarn
Overbody:	Yellow or olive chenille
Fantail:	Cock pheasant neck feather

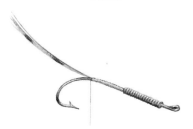

1. Wrap hook shank, tie in several pheasant tail fibers to represent antennae, and then wrap the front 2/3 of hook with heavy lead wire.

2. Choose a bunch of brown deer hair selected from the base of a bucktail, and tie one bunch directly over the antennae. Tie in a second bunch to extend past the hook eye as shown, and secure yet a third bunch underneath the hook eye. Bind all hair smoothly and cement winds.

3. At rear of hook, and on each side of the antennae, tie in a small bunch of brown bucktail to represent claws. These should be slightly shorter than the antennae and separated by about 30 degrees.

The habitat range of crayfish (or crawdads if you prefer) almost perfectly matches that in which we find bass. This cousin of the lobster is a familiar bait to most fishermen, and the flyrodder has found a variety of ways to replicate these crustaceans with fur, feathers and such.

When constructing crayfish imitations, particular attention must be directed toward the following features. First, crayfish are found on the bottom of lakes, ponds, and streams; some form of weight is usually desirable, and a weed guard might also be added. Second, crayfish swim backwards when disturbed, and most crayfish patterns are designed as illustrated, with the head tied at the back of the hook. Third, improper construction technique can easily upset the balance of most crayfish imitations causing them to twist during retrieval, thus reducing their effectiveness. This is remedied by paying careful attention to balance at the tying bench, and even by testing your flies in the bathtub. The most common problem is usually associated with claws which act as unbalanced rudders.

Crayfish vary widely in size throughout the year; their growth rate is related to their habitat, together with the individual species' characteristics. Color, too, will vary, although it is generally agreed that their coloration usually matches that of their environment. Those crayfish that have molted recently will reveal distinctly lighter hues.

Fishing crayfish imitations is usually best at dusk or at night when the naturals become more active. A slow retrieve along the bottom, interspersed with a darting fast strip of a foot or so, will often prove to be the combination which will fool all types of bass.

DAVE'S CRAYFISH
(Dave Whitlock)

Hook:	4X long, sizes 2 to 8
Thread:	To match body color
Pincers:	Two pairs of hen rump feathers
Eyes:	Pair of melted nylon monofilament beads
Antennae:	Two peccary fibers
Underbody:	Synthetic dubbing
Legs:	Soft grizzly hackle
Overbody & Tail:	Swiss straw
Rib:	Copper, brass or gold wire

SWIMMING CRAYFISH
(Byron Yarrington)

Hook:	Salmon, bronze or black, sizes 2 to 6
Thread:	Tan monocord
Weight:	Heavy lead wire
Body:	Tan chenille
Antennae:	Ringneck pheasant tail fibers
Claws:	Two bunches of brown bucktail
Legs:	Ringneck pheasant body feather
Tail & Back:	Brown bucktail from base of tail

TED'S CRAYFISH
(Ted Godfrey)

Hook:	2X long, sizes 2 to 10
Thread:	Brown
Weight:	Heavy lead wire
Rib:	Brown thread
Underbody:	Light brown deer body hair
Overbody:	Red squirrel tail
Thorax:	Olive chenille
Eyes:	Beads of melted monofilament
Claws:	Ringneck pheasant body feathers
Legs:	Ringneck pheasant rump feather

4. Select a large ringneck pheasant body feather from the lower center of the back, and tie in by the tip as shown. When pulled forward you'll want the individual fibers to curve downward. Attach a 12 inch piece of tan chenille.

5. Cover hook shank with 2 wraps of chenille, trim excess, move thread to center of body and fold the pheasant feather toward the hook eye, securing in the center. Next pull the rear bunch of bucktail over the pheasant feather, taking care not to disturb the antennae, claws, or legs.

6. Locate thread about 1/4" from hook eye. Select both the top and bottom bucktail bunches and separately fold them toward the rear, securing at your thread location. Trim the bottom bunch, leaving about 1/2" to represent a folded tail. Finish by binding the top bunch to the center.

DRY FLIES

 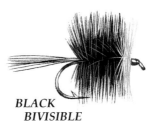 

GREY   WHITE   BLACK   BROWN
WULFF   WULFF   BIVISIBLE   BIVISIBLE

The upright wing dry fly is customarily associated with the mayfly imitations used by trout fishermen, and the hairwing Wulff style fly, originated by Lee Wulff, has become a standard. Armed with the patterns listed here, in sizes 6 to 12, the bass fisherman will be prepared for the hatches of larger mayflies found in warmwater lakes and streams

	Tail	Body	Wing	Hackle
Black Wulff	Moose body	Pink floss	Moose body	Black
Brown Wulff	Brown	Cream	Brown	Brown
Gray Wulff	Brown bucktail	Gray fur	Brown bucktail	Blue dun gray
Grizzly Wulff	Brown bucktail	Yellow floss	Brown bucktail	Grizzly
White Wulff	White bucktail	Cream spun fur	White bucktail	Badger

For a high-floating, simple-to-tie and easily seen dry fly, the bivisible ranks high among today's popular dry flies. Constructed entirely of dry fly quality rooster hackle, the front portion of this design features several turns of white hackle as a visibility aid for the fisherman. For bass and panfish tie this pattern on standard dry fly hooks in sizes 6 to 14 .

	Tail	Body Hackle	Front Hackle
Black Bivisible	Black	Black	White
Blue Dun Bivisible	Blue dun	Blue dun	White
Brown Bivisible	Brown	Brown	White
Ginger Bivisible	Ginger	Ginger	White

Standard dry fly hooks are normally used when tying bivisibles. Some tyers prefer this fly without a tail.

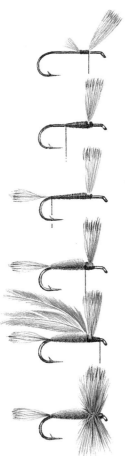

1.   Secure the tying thread and form a wing base. Select a bunch of brown bucktail, align the tips, and tie tightly on top of the hook shank.

2.   Raise the bucktail wing and hold it upright while making several tight turns of thread directly in front of the wing. Next, divide the wings taking several figure-8 thread wraps. Cut off butt ends on a taper.

3.   Select another bunch of bucktail and secure at rear on top of the hook shank forming the tail. Again, trim the butt ends on a taper to provide a smooth foundation for the body.

4.   Beginning at the tail, wrap or dub a gray muskrat fur body.

5.   Select 2 or 3 blue dun gray hackles, remove webby portion at base, and tie on, convex sides together.

6.   Wrap one hackle, keeping most of the wraps behing the wing. Wrap the second hackle, placing most wraps ahead of the wing. Trim away excess butt ends, form head and whip finish.

1.   Attach thread, wrap a base the entire length of he hook shank. Select a small bunch of stiff hackle barbs and attach, forming the tail.

2.   Select a long, stiff dry fly hackle of the desired color, remove fuzz and webby portion, and attach by the butt end. (Some tyers prefer the tapered appearance which results from attaching the tip end.)

3.   Wrap hackle forward in tight, closely spaced turns. Tie down securely and trim away excess.

4.   Select and tie in a second hackle, and repeat step 3. This should result in the hackle covering about 80% of the hook shank. On larger hooks a 3rd hackle may be needed.

5.   Now, select a white dry fly hackle, just slightly larger than the hackles previously chosen, and tie in at the front.

6.   Wrap 2 or 3 turns of the white hackle, tie off, trim away excess, and whip finish.

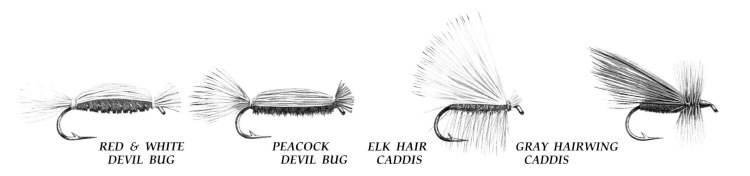

RED & WHITE DEVIL BUG **PEACOCK DEVIL BUG** **ELK HAIR CADDIS** **GRAY HAIRWING CADDIS**

For the beginner this fly, sometimes known as a Cooper Bug or Doodle Bug , is one of the easiest to construct and can be tied in a wide variety of colors. Most often natural gray/brown deer body hair is used on top while a variety of materials, mostly chenille, serve for the body. Try this fly in sizes 6 to 10 tied on a 1X or 2X long dry fly hook.

Downwing dry flies are those which have wings extending flat over their body. Such flies usually represent caddisflies or stoneflies, both common aquatic insects. Some larger species skitter or flutter on the water, driving the resident bass into a feeding spree. Either Al Troth's Elk Caddis or the Hairwing Caddis will serve well in sizes 6 to 12.

	Body	*Wing*	*Hackle*
Brown Elk Caddis	*Brown*	*Lt. Elk*	*Brown*
Olive Elk Caddis	*Olive*	*Lt. Elk*	*Brown*
Black Hairwing Caddis	*Black*	*Black*	*Black*
Brown Hairwing Caddis	*Brown-olive*	*Dark tan*	*Ginger*
Gray Hairwing Caddis	*Gray-olive*	*Gray*	*Blue dun*

1.   Place hook in vise, attach thread, and attach a length of chenille (or peacock herl), having first stripped the fuzz from the end being secured.

2.   Wrap chenille forward to a point 1/8 inch behind the hook eye. Tie down securely and trim away excess.

3.   Return the thread to the rear of the body by either tying off and restarting at the back, or by simply making wide spaced turns over the body.

4.   Select a bunch of deer body hair, align the tips, and tie down firmly at the rear of the hook. Keep the hair on top and move your tying thread forward in wide turns over the body.

5.   With one hand pull the deer body hair to the front and secure it tightly in front as shown.

6.   Tie off with half hitches or whip finish. The butt ends of deer hair should be trimmed to extend just past the hook eye. A flexible cement will make the fly more durable.

1.   Attach thread, wrap a base, and attach a dry fly hackle at the rear.

2.   Make a body of fur dubbing to extend forward about 2/3rds length of hook shank.

3.   Wrap hackle forward in wide turns (palmer fashion) to the front end of the body.

4.   Trim hackle from the top of the body.

5.   Apply a wing of elk body hair as shown. Be sure to keep the elk hair tips even as you cut them from the hide. The hair will flare when tied down. Be sure to keep it on top of the hook.

6.   Whip finish to complete the fly. Trim the butt ends as shown, and apply cement.

FROGS

When it comes to the subject of lures for bass fishing, one of the first categories to come to mind is frogs. There are probably more types of fly rod frogs than there are pages in this book. All boil down to an attempt to simulate the basic size, shape, action, and colors of the natural frog. The fisherman should keep in mind that the majority of frogs are not huge and stout like bullfrogs, rather most are no bigger than your thumb, and may appear quite skinny when outstretched in the water. Also, when viewed from a fish's perspective from below, most are very light colored on the underside. Rather than show all the different combinations possible, here are the very basic construction techniques leading from a simple, impressionistic frog design to the more complex and realistic varieties.

1. Begin by spinning deer body hair over the rear 1/3 of the hook shank, pack tightly, and trim to shape.

2. From a bucktail select 2 bunches for legs and tie on in front of the spun deer hair so that the butt ends extend rearward, half on each side.

3. Trim away excess bucktail, resume spinning deer body hair over front 2/3 of the hook, tie off and trim remaining body to shape.

4. Using a heavier thread (size D) or wire, wrap around the bucktail legs to form a knee, and then overwrap the first layer of thread (or wire).

Front legs may be added by securing two small bunches of bucktail in position; be careful not to cut them when trimming the surrounding deer body hair.

An alternative for front legs is to use a small bunch of rubber hackle strands. Making an overhand knot results in a realistic appearance.

The simple bucktail hind legs may be enhanced by winding a "knee joint" of thread. Wire may inserted into the leg or used to wrap the bend.

By tying on a separate cut-off hook shank or wire, individual, movable, legs can be made and attached to the hook using wire or monofilament loops.

Rubber strands may be used to create a very effective, yet simple set of rear legs. An overhand knot forms the bended knee.

Eyes are added by making a flat spot with a razor blade to which doll eyes may be glued; or sockets can be formed with a woodburning tool.

Solid plastic eyes with an attached stem, or even cut-off hat pins, or beads, or bead chain, painted as eyes, may be glued into the trimmed deer body hair.

Tim England showed us ultimate realism by using 1 1/2 doll eyes, glued back to back, and inserted into sockets cut into the deer body hair.

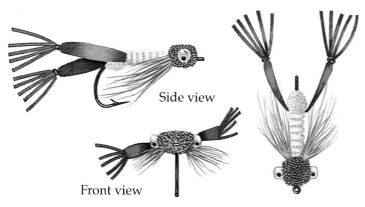

WIGGLE LEGS FROG (Dave Whitlock)

Side view

Front view

Top view

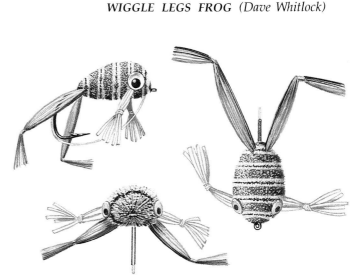

SANG SINKING FROG (Peter Sang)

27

Eelworm Streamer

D ave Whitlock, working upon patterns previously developed by Larry Green and Bill Greenway, designed the now-standard Eelworm Streamer—"a fly-rodder's answer to the plastic worm and/or the jig-and-eel bass lures."

Tied with long flexible saddle hackle which will undulate in the water, the weighted head and weed guard permit fishing this fly deep around the hiding places of big bass.

Usual fishing techniques call for a slow, erratic retrieve along the bottom, normally using a sink-tip flyline. The heavily weighted head makes this fly act much like a jig, and the tail waves enticingly as the head bounces upward and downward.

Favorite colors for bass are blue, black, purple, brown , olive and yellow, and are the colors most often used for the Eelworm Streamer. However, the fly tyer should feel free to select his own favorite color combination.

Hook: *Mustad 36890 or similar, sizes 6 through 3/0.*
Thread: *Black monocord and red or fluorescent red/orange thread.*
Eyes: *Bead chain or lead dumb - bell eyes.*
Weight: *Lead wire, if needed.*
Tail: *Four narrow, dyed grizzly saddle hackles with flexible stems, plus two shorter matching saddle hackles, one half the length of the first four.*
Rib: *Softer grizzly neck or saddle hackle to match the tail color.*
Body: *A dubbing mix of 50% orlon and 50% natural fur such as rabbit. Colors to match and blend with the tail colors.*

1. Affix a thread base, attach weed guard material, add bead chain eyes using figure-8 wraps, and add lead wire for weight. (Lead eyes eliminate the need for the extra weight.)

2. Separate the 4 saddle hackles into 2 matching pairs, and place so the concave sides of one pair faces the other. Their length should be about 3 times the shank length.

3. Add the 2 shorter saddle hackles, one on each side, and set to curve outward. These are 1/2 the length of the others.

4. Tie in the softer hackle (or 2) which will be used as a rib.

5. Apply a thickly dubbed body wrapping forward to the eyes of the fly.

6. Spiral the ribbing hackle forward to the eyes, secure, and cut away surplus.

7. More dubbing is wrapped in figure-8's around the eyes to form a large head.

8. Complete by securing the weed guard. Change to red thread and wrap a head, adding a bright spot to the fly.

GRASSHOPPERS

Late each summer, and extending into autumn, grasshoppers can be found in the weeds and fields adjacent to many of our warmwater ponds and rivers. When in abundance, there is always a small number of these 'hoppers that accidentally fall into the water and become meals for bass and panfish alike. This is especially true on windy days as breezes carry these insects for unusual distances. Many a youngster has teased a fish from its hiding place by drifting live grasshoppers down a meadow stream. Flyfishermen replicate this with their imitations, and have learned that these large flys are best cast so that they hit the water with a resounding "plop." Grasshopper coloration varies greatly, but yellow bodied flies seem to work best.

JOE'S HOPPER

LETORT HOPPER
(Ed Shenk)

DAVE'S HOPPER
(Dave Whitlock)

1. Using a 2X or 3X long hook, attach thread and add a tail of red hackle fibers.

2. Attach yellow acrylic yarn (or Orlon), plus a long brown hackle. Some tyers prefer the new floating foam for their grasshopper bodies.

3. Wrap yarn body 2/3rds way forward, secure and trim away excess.

4. Palmer (spiral forward) the hackle in evenly spaced turns over the yarn body.

5. Trim hackle to short stubs.

6. Affix an underwing on top the body using a small bunch of brown bucktail, dyed red and extending to the end of the tail.

7. Cut a segment from a mottled turkey wing quill, coat with adhesive to prevent splitting, and trim to shape shown. Tie on directly over the bucktail underwing.

8. Make a pair of "hopper legs" by cutting segments from a large mottled turkey wing quill, then forming the jointed leg shape with a simple overhand knot. Tie in one leg on each side of the body.

9. Using natural brown deer body hair dyed yellow, spin a bunch directly in front of the body, keeping the natural tips pointed toward the rear.

10. Spin additional clumps of deer body hair to complete the head, tie off and trim, being sure not to cut away the natural tips which form the collar of the fly.

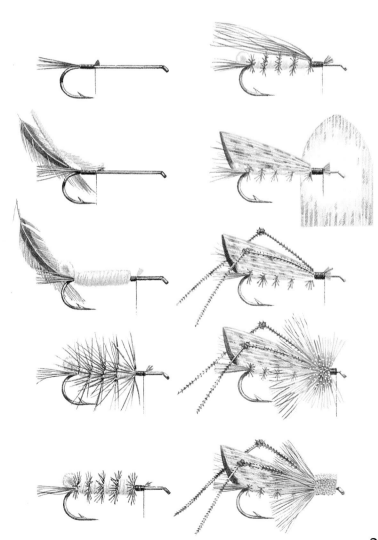

HAIRBUGS

FRONT

TOP

Hook:	Stinger style hook in all sizes
Thread:	To match body color
Tail:	A bunch of marabou fibers, plus 2 or three wide hackle feathers on each side.
Skirt:	A hackle to match the tail hackles
Body:	Deer body hair
Legs:	Rubber hackle

1. Place hook in vise and attach monofilament weedguard material. This should be tied about halfway down the bend.

2. Strip a bunch of marabou fibers of the desired color and secure them to the hook with 5 or 6 turns of thread. Trim away excess.

3. Match up two or three pairs of soft, wide, neck or back hackles of the desired colors. Arrange so that each pair, with convex sides together, splays outward as shown.

Hairbugs, in their many forms, represent the archetype of 20th century bass flies. Earlier bass flies were often just oversize versions of traditional trout fly patterns. The hairbug, however, soon became firmly identified with bass fishing and, in addition to the pattern types shown on this page, one must include the frog, mice and moth designs in the category known as hairbugs. The hairbug shown here essentially follows the design of Dave Whitlock's Most Whit Hairbug series. Many fly tyers have developed procedures, styles and variations on the theme of the hairbug, and a few are shown on this page.

When tying this type of fly the liberal use of an adhesive cement is advisable. A firm cement on the face of the hairbug will stiffen it so that your fly will behave more like a popper. The doll eyes, which at first glance seem merely decorative, can add a critical degree of additional flotation when properly applied. Many bass flyrodders recommend keeping your hairbugs sparse to minimize air resistance while casting.

Deer hair is more water absorbant than cork or balsa, so many bass fishermen prefer these materials over deer hair. Fly tyers, on the other hand, seem to thoroughly enjoy all the different applications of deer hair, and their creations have sure brought a lot of bass to net.

BLACK RUBBERTAIL
(Tim England)

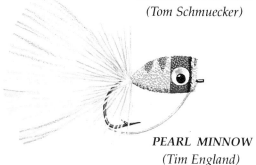

SCHMUECKER BUG
(Tom Schmuecker)

PEARL MINNOW
(Tim England)

4. Select a matching or complimentary hackle. Attach this at the tail and wrap 3 or 4 turns directly over the previous tie-in point. Secure and trim excess. At this time it's a good idea to fold this skirt toward the back and bind down with a few wraps of thread or wire. This gets these fibers out of harm's way while trimming later on.

5. Begin the body by selecting a clump of deer body hair and spinning it in place, immediately in front of the skirt hackle. Pack tight and repeat this process until the rear third of the hook shank is covered.

6. Attach a strand of rubber hackle directly in front of the deer body hair, allowing at least 2 inches extending on each side.

7. Repeat the previous steps by spinning other deer hair bunches, add another piece of rubber hackle, and finally spin a face of white (or bright) deer body hair to help make your hairbug more visible. You may alternate different colors of hair to obtain any effect desired.

8. Using a single edge razor blade, or scissors, trim to the shape shown. To avoid cutting the rubber hackle fold it to the back before proceeding. If doll eyes are to be used cut a flat spot on each side to create a base.

9. The trimmed shape should look like this. Cement the eyes in place and bring the mono-filament forward and complete the weedguard. Trim the rubber hackle to the desired length, and generously cement the face of the bug to improve stiffness.

JIGS

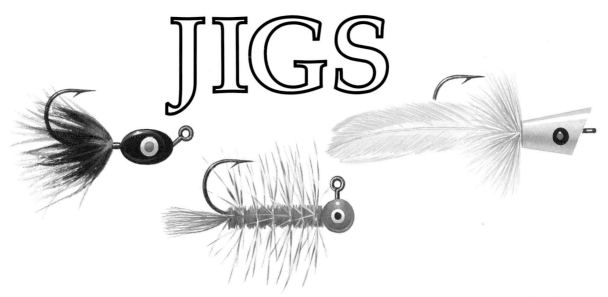

Possibly the most overlooked of the flyrod lures would be the simple weighted jig. For some it might be that the lead head, which defines all jigs, makes it seem cumbersome with a fly rod. This may be true for the larger sizes, however, in small sizes this is one of the deadliest lures for a great many gamefish—especially bass. And, what could be simpler to construct? All you need are some pre-made jig hooks, or you can make your own. Add your choice of bucktail, synthetic hair, feathers, or marabou (my favorite), secure with some half hitches, cement for durability, and paint your preferred colors. The jig design makes it sink quickly and forces the hook to ride upside down making it almost weedless. Be sure to have some all white, all black, all yellow, and red and white jigs in a variety of sizes for bass and panfish alike.

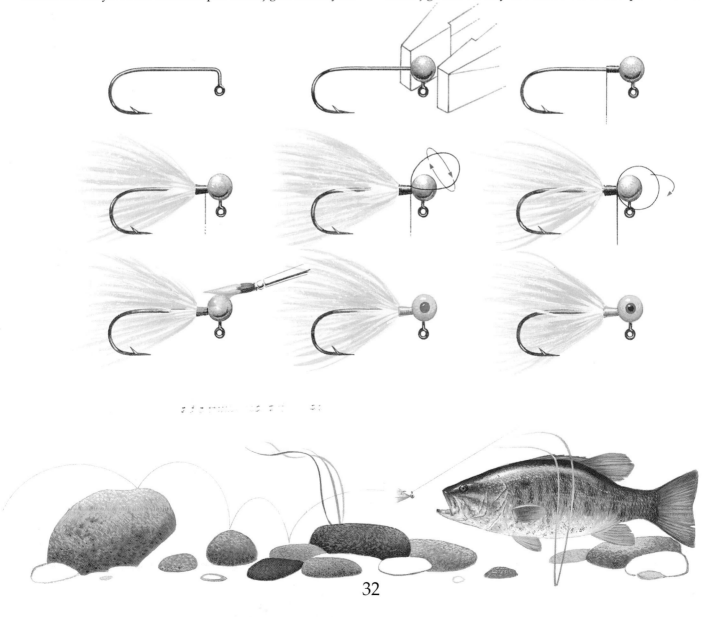

leeches

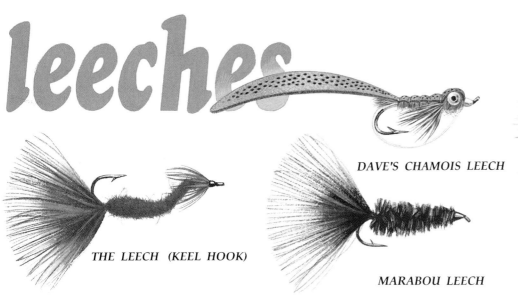

DAVE'S CHAMOIS LEECH

THE LEECH (KEEL HOOK)

MARABOU LEECH

THE LEECH

One of the more disreputable aquatic characters must certainly be the lowly leech, so common to freshwater ponds and lakes throughout the United States. The human aversion to this creature is not shared by bass, however, which see leeches as a dinner opportunity. Thus, a number of fly patterns have evolved to represent the variety of leeches, the natural color of which varies from almost black to a mottled light tan, often with shades of red-brown and olive in evidence. Since leeches are usually found near the bottom, imitations are often weighted and fished slowly, in almost a crawling manner, casting toward shore and retrieving into deeper water.

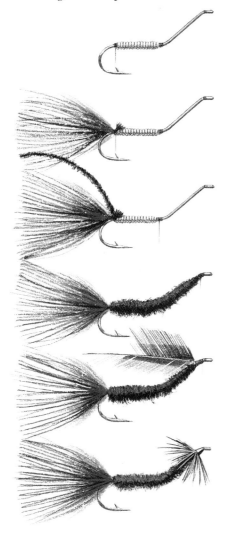

1. Secure the hook in the vise and bend to the shape shown. Attach thread at rear. Lead wire for weight should be wrapped on at this time.

2. Strip a large bunch of fibers from the stem of a marabou plume dyed black, and tie on as a tail.

3. At the rear of the hook attach a length of black mohair yarn, or coarse wool.

4. Wrap the yarn forward, tapering the body as shown.

5. Attach a soft black hen hackle at the front of the body.

6. Make 2 turns of hackle to form the collar, tie off, cut away excess, and finish the head.

THE LEECH
(Thom Green)

Hook: 3X long, sizes 4 to 10
Thread: Color of body
Tail: Marabou, color to match body
Body: Mohair or dubbing, black, claret, brown or olive
Hackle: Soft hen hackle

DAVE'S CHAMOIS LEECH
(Dave Whitlock)

Hook: Black salmon, sizes 4 to 10
Thread: Color of body
Rib: Wire
Body: Coarse dubbing, black, brown, tan or olive, a shade lighter than the chamois strip overbody
Tail: Short red wool
Overbody: Long chamois strip, about 3 times hook length, tied in at front of hook and secured over the body by the wraps of the wire rib.
Collar: Soft hen hackle
Eyes: Optional, made of bead chain

MARABOU LEECH

Hook: 3X long, sizes 2 to10
Thread: Black
Tail: Black marabou
Body: Black marabou, either wound and trimmed, or layered on the shank
Hackle: Soft black hen hackle (optional)
Comment: Several fly tyers have designed variations of this basic pattern. Use your imagination and experiment; marabou gives the fly lots of movement.

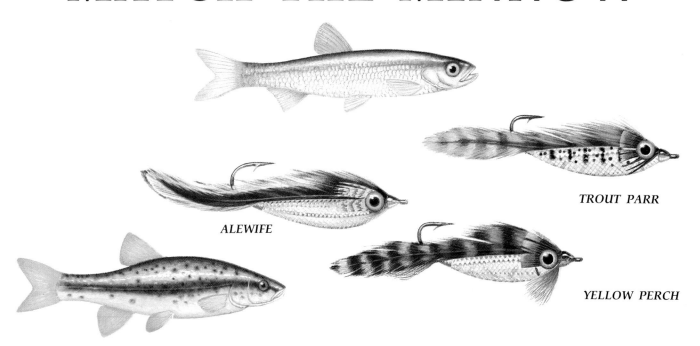

ALEWIFE

TROUT PARR

YELLOW PERCH

Modern glues and cements have permitted fly designers to experiment with new and unique fly construction methods. Cements reduce the tyer's dependency on thread to secure and bind the fly's components, thereby liberating fly tying from the constraints which necessitated thread for so many years. Many tyers have used epoxy cements, cyanoacrylate glues (also known as CA or Super glues) and even hot-melt glues. The progress of such experimentation can be traced through the new designs reported in the books and magazines during the 1970's and 1980's, and one such design result is Dave Whitlock's "Match-the-Minnow" series, a still-evolving group of realistic baitfish imitations.

Essential to this series is Dave's use of modern glues to bond a pair of hackles along the entire body length, together with the ability to attach the small eyes directly to the minnow's Mylar body. Thread is still used to secure the body and bind the butt ends of all feathers, thereby retaining much of the traditional aesthetics of fly design.

Specific choices of colors and materials may be selected to produce imitations which resemble virtually any baitfish. The best recommendation would be to match the colors of minnows where you expect to be fishing. Then again, these methods may also be used to produce a series of bright attractor flies for bass which will be semi-weedless due to the upside-down hook.

1. With the hook secured upside down in your vise, place a pre-cut body form of aluminum, lead tape or plastic, and cement in place.

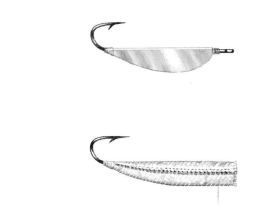

2. Slide a length of flattened Mylar tubing over the body form and secure at rear. Tie off and restart your thread at the head position.

3. Secure the Mylar tubing in front and trim away excess. Select a 2 to 4 hackles, place concave sides together, and tie at top of head so they extend beyond the bend as shown.

4. Choose two small, soft, breast feathers of the desired color to represent the head and gill covers. Tie in, one on each side, at the head.

5. Wrap a smooth head and tie off. Now, using a CA glue, cement the hackles along the top of the body, full length, cement body and winds, and add eyes directly behind the head.

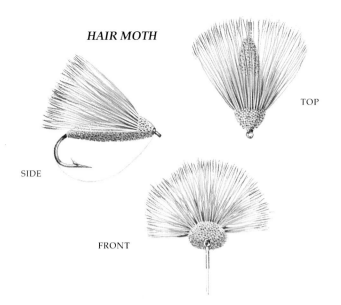

HAIR MOTH

TOP

SIDE

FRONT

Moths

Top view shows the widespread hair representing the outstretched wings trapped in the water's surface.

By trimming the moth flat along the bottom, the entire wing outline is revealed from underwater.

Some of the earliest bass lures included flies which imitated the various moths which so commonly find themselves inadvertently trapped in the water's surface. These moths, usually with both wings outstretched in the surface film, will quiver and shudder sending out a series of vibrations and ripples which will catch the attention of any bass in the neighborhood. Commonly, the fisherman should cast these flies into the openings of weed beds, let them sit quietly, then by wiggling the fly rod tip, transmit motion to the imitation. This technique is especially effective at night when moths are most active.

FEATHERWING MOTH

HENSHALL BUG

GERBUBBLE BUG

HENSHALL BUG - One of the oldest, most effective of bass flies. The tail and wing are often tied with calf tail.
GERBUBBLE BUG - Originally constructed from balsa wood or cork, it may also be tied with deer body hair. Soft hackles extending along each side (or better yet, marabou) result in a fly which quivers and vibrates with each small movement of the flyrod.
FEATHERWING MOTH - The most realistic of the standard moth patterns. The cork or foam body is topped with rounded goose shoulder feathers. One limitation is its tendency to twist when being cast.

1. Attach thread, wrap a thread base the full length of the shank, and attach a monofilament weedguard as shown.

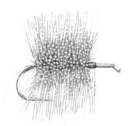

2. Beginning at the rear, tightly spin several bunches of deer body hair until you've covered 2/3rds of the hook shank. Half hitch to secure thread.

3. Remove the fly from the vise and trim the moth body to a full cigar shape as illustrated. Return fly to the vise.

4. Make sure you have a firm thread base on the front 1/3 of the hook, and stack 2 or 3 bunches of deer body hair on the top and sides of the hook shank. The hair tips should extend just past the hook bend.

5. Trim the butt ends of the deer body hair as shown.

6. Bring the weedguard forward and secure. Cement both the thread windings and the deer hair body.

WHIT'S MOUSE RAT

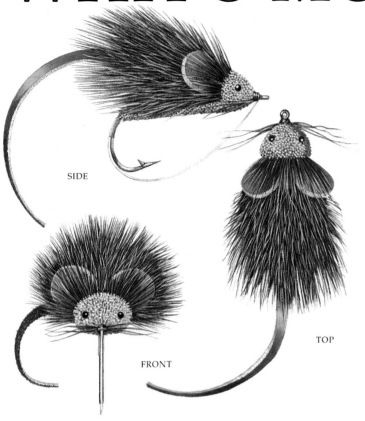

SIDE

TOP

FRONT

For years the mouse has been one of the fun flies often tackled by fly tyers once they've learned the basics of spinning deer body hair. Many of these creations, however, have ended up decorating hats or have been used to tease family members when placed in the corner of a room. This should not be their only use since the mouse imitation has proved to be a very effective bass fly, especially when teased, across the water's surface at dusk, or even well after dark. Earlier versions lacked the chamois leather ears; usually the eyes were simply painted on, and often the tail was just a piece of rubber band, but these features are usually of greater concern to the fisherman than they are to the fish. While most other patterns of the mouse require that the entire body be trimmed to shape, Dave Whitlock's version, the Mouserat, requires that the deer body hair be tied in such a manner that the natural tips of the deer body hair remain, and no trimming is needed on the top part of the fly body. This is achieved by stacking, rather than spinning, the hair with the tips pointed rearward. It may be necessary to align the tips of the deer hair before applying it to the hook.

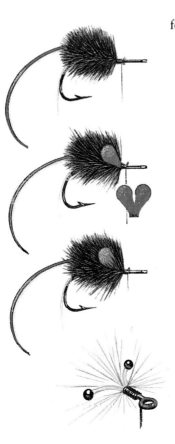

1. Attach monofilament for a weed guard, tie on a tail cut from a strip of chamois, and on top of the hook stack several bunches of dark deer body hair (cut short on the underside). Cover 2/3rds of hook shank.

2. Cut a piece of chamois as shown and secure on top of the hook to form the ears of the mouse.

3. Spin another bunch of deer body hair directly in front of the ears.

4. The optional eyes can be added at this time. Use either mono-filament which has been melted into a ball at one end, or preformed eyes, and tie to hook.

5. One more bunch of deer body hair is spun in front of the eyes.

6. Remove hook from the vise, trim flat on bottom along the entire length. Next, trim to shape beginning at the nose and working back to the ears.

7. Replace hook in vise and tie in, tips pointing to the rear, 8 strands of dark moose mane or similar coarse hair. Using figure 8 wraps, divide these whiskers with half extending from each side.

8. Bring weedguard forward to complete.

MUDDLERS

Ever since its creation by Don Gapen for his fishing in Ontario, the Muddler Minnow has probably been the subject of more fly fishing articles than any other fly. Although the original Gapen Muddler was not as fancy as its construction in the examples shown here, its effectiveness has never been questioned. Whether tied in small sizes for trout or panfish, or in larger sizes for bass and salmon, the Muddler Minnow in all its variations remains one of the great flyfishing lures, deserving of a place in every fly box. Probably it is the design, rather than a particular size or color combination, that contributes to the Muddler's success. The spun deer hair head seems to cause the fly to move in a lifelike manner. In addition to the designs shown here, other color combinations, especially in black or yellow, have been used successfully. Even a trolling pattern, some 4 to 5 inches long, has been effective for smallmouth bass.

Another variation on the original design includes adding weight under the tinsel body and substituting chenille or wool for the deer hair head. These changes result in a quick-sinking version, ideal for fishing along the bottom.

MUDDLER MINNOW

MIZZOLIAN SPOOK

WHITE MARABOU MUDDLER

MULTICOLOR MARABOU MUDDLER

RABBIT FUR MUDDLER

MUDDLER MINNOW

Hook:	2X or 3X long
Thread:	Black
Tail:	Mottled turkey
Body:	Flat gold tinsel
Underwing:	Grey squirrel tail
Wing:	Mottled turkey
Collar & Head:	Natural deer body hair

1.   Attach thread at rear and tie tail on top of hook. Bring thread about 2/3rds of the way to the front and tie in a length of flat gold tinsel.

2.   Wrap the tinsel toward the tail in close, even wraps. Once you've reached the tail, wrap forward over the first layer of tinsel. Stop at the origination point, tie off, and trim excess.

3.   Take a small clump of squirrel tail (or other hair) and tie on top at the front of the body. This hair should extend to the bend of the hook. Cement to improve durability.

4.   Match two sections from a pair of mottled turkey wing quills and, with their concave sides together, tie directly on top of the underwing.

5.   Select a small bunch of deer body hair, leaving the natural tips in place, and spin in front of the wing. The tips should be positioned so they point toward the rear, while the cut butt ends point forward.

6.   Spin one or two more bunches of deer body hair in front to complete the head. Trim to the shape shown, being sure not to trim away those tip ends which form the collar.

Nymphs

In the unseen depths of every lake, pond, river, and stream lies the aquatic food chain which supports the gamefish we pursue. The adult insects are a familiar sight to fishermen—mayflies, caddisflies, dragonflies, damselflies, stoneflies, aquatic moths, mosquitoes, midges, and so forth. Not so familiar perhaps, are the immature stages of these insects, most commonly refered to as "nymphs" although sometimes labelled as "larvae" and/or "pupae." The nymphal stage of insects is of enormous impor-

tance to the fisherman because these food forms constitute a large portion of the diet of immature bass, and a continual source of nourishment to mature fish. At times, during a major insect hatching period, the nymphs become available in such abundance that they will trigger heavy feeding sprees, particularly in the case of smallmouth bass. The nymphs tied for bass fishing are usually designed to be more impressionistic than realistic, to impart a sense of motion, and to be durable.

DAMSEL FLY • The familiar damselfly, or darner, selects aquatic weeds and grasses for its preferred habitat. The slender nymphs tend toward muted tan, cream or olive, unlike the bright metallic colors of the adult insects.

DRAGON FLY • The straight and slender adult bears little resemblance to the plump form of most nymphs. Brown, olive and gray imitations are best retrieved just over the top of weed beds.

HELLGRAMMITE • At least the artificial fly can't pinch like a live hellgrammite. These brownish-black nymphs hatch from lakes and streams to become large dobsonflies.

MAYFLY • Only the larger species are of interest to bass, and these usually are the burrowing types which favor a mud or soft bottom. When they hatch, it is often in large quantities.

STONEFLY • Almost always found in fast moving, highly oxygenated water containing rocks, stones or boulders. The black, brown, or yellow nymphs, which grow to over two inches long, may live as long as 3 years underwater.

STONEFLY NYMPH

DRAGON FLY NYMPH

LARGE MAYFLY NYMPH

Damselfly

DAVE'S DAMSEL (*Dave Whitlock*)
Hook: *2X long, sizes 2 to 12*
Thread: *To match body color*
Tail: *Short tuft of marabou*
Body: *Nylon floss*
Legs: *Soft hackle wrapped over front 1/3 of body*
Wingpad: *Nylon raffia (Swiss Straw) tied in 1/3 way back and pulled forward over top*
Eyes:*Bead chain*

Dragonfly

DREDGEBUG (*Dick Stewart*)
Hook: *3X or 4X long*
Thread: *To match body color, usually grey, olive or tan*
Weight: *Lead wire if needed*
Body: *Wool or dubbing tied full*
Wingpad: *Short mallard flank feather tied on top, color to match body*
Legs: *Soft hackle wrapped in front of body, to fold backwards*
Head: *3 or 4 wraps of chenille*
Eyes:*Lead dumbbell (optional)*

Hellgrammite

UGLY HELGY (*Dick Stewart*)
Hook: *4X long, sizes 2 to 8*
Thread: *Black or brown*
Weight: *Lead wire wrapped full length of hook shank*
Tail: *4 pieces of black ostrich herl, 2/3 body length*
Body: *Brown chenille*
Rib: *Black ostrich herl, length of body*
Legs: *Sections of black ostrich herl, 2 on each side, 1/2 body length*

Mayfly

DRAKE NYMPH (*Dick Stewart*)
Hook: *4X long, sizes 6 to 10*
Thread: *To match body color*
Tail: *Short tuft of marabou*
Body: *A dubbing mix to match natural, usually dark tan, thicker at the thorax*
Legs: *Two turns of soft mottled brown hen rump hackle over front 1/3 of body*
Wingpad: *Brown goose quill segment tied in 1/3 way back and pulled forward over the thorax*

Stonefly

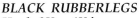

BLACK RUBBERLEGS
Hook: *3X or 4X long*
Thread: *Black*
Weight: *Lead wire*
Tail: *2 strands of gray rubber*
Body: *Black chenille*
Legs: *3 strands of gray rubber, tied so there are 3 legs extending from each side*
Antennae: *two strands of gray rubber hackle*
Comment: *The Girdle bug is similar but with white rubber.*

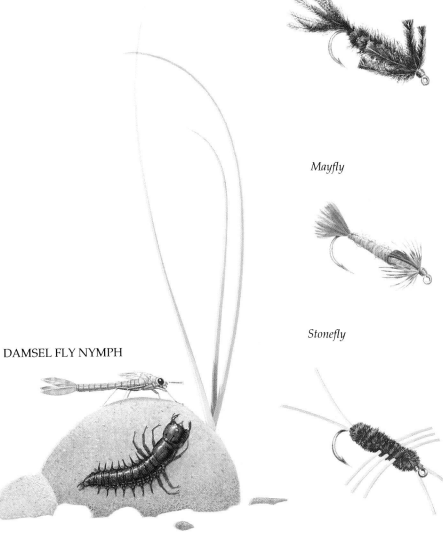

DAMSEL FLY NYMPH

HELLGRAMMITE

Poppers

I must leave it to the hairsplitters to to determine whether or not hard bodied lures are properly included in the category of flies. I know however, that these cork or balsa wood creations were a part of my earliest bass fishing, and they've accounted for an impressive number of smallmouth bass. These lures are easy to make and can be produced at home in a variety of sizes, styles, and colors. Unless you've spent some time casting and retrieving poppers it might be difficult to appreciate the subtle differences between the various styles. Lefty Kreh once wrote "making bass bugs is as precise as tying a cut wing or building a nymph." Listed below are the six basic poppers, together with a brief description of their individual characteristics. Take care in the making and your poppers will function better.

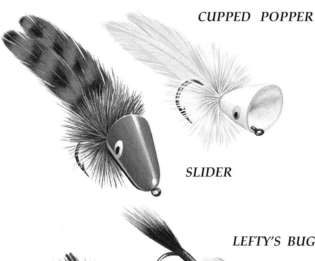

CUPPED POPPER

SLIDER

LEFTY'S BUG

PENCIL POPPER

SKIPPING BUG

GERBUBBLE BUG

The deep-cupped face of this, the standard and best-known style of popper, produces a lot of surface disturbance (a popping) when retrieved. This cupping may cause the fly to dive underwater a bit occasionally making the casting pick-up a bit more difficult.

This is the quietest of all the cork body lures and can be subtly inched around lily pads, weeds, and such. Sometimes called a Sneaky Pete type lure, it's often a favorite on windless, glassy surfaces.

This bug results from Lefty Kreh's many years of guiding smallmouth bass fishermen on the Potomac River. Note its features: low hook position, high visibility, minimal tail, a flat face and bottom, and plenty of hook clearance.

For a minnow-like surface lure the Pencil Popper has proved effective and is a bit less wind resistant when casting. Try this when minnows are schooling, or below dams where injured baitfish are common.

The name suggests the action of this bug. The slanted face forces it to skip across the water surface, a particularly useful feature on windy days. Also the skipping action might suggest the behavoir of a minnow under attack.

The hackle tail, and hackle on each side, all sandwiched between two church-window shaped pieces of cork or balsa. Some bass fishermen believe an improvement on the original design is to substitute marabou for the hackle, giving it lots more motion.

1   Select a hook from one of the styles designed with some form of bend or kink to help prevent the cork body from turning once in place.

2   Using a saw, file knife and sandpaper, shape your cork (or balsa wood) to the desired shape. Usually you will want to keep it flat along the bottom.

3   Cut a slit lengthwise along the bottom with a coping saw, hacksaw blade, craft saw, or razor blade.

4   Fill the slot with epoxy and position the cork on the hook shank. Remember, align the cork so the shank is in the lower half, making certain it doesn't interfere with the point. Allow epoxy to set.

5   Add tail and/or skirt of hair, feathers, or such. Rubber legs may be added by threading a needle with rubber and inserting with pliers through the cork. Fill slot with epoxy mixed with cork dust.

6   Paint the body using acrylic hobby or artist's paints. This will seal and waterproof the body, making it more durable. Once dry, follow with a coat of decoupage glaze for a nicer finish.

7   Push a small nail in a cork, and a straight pin in the opposite end. Then dip the nail in paint and place a round spot where you want an eye. The pin can be used to form a pupil.

8   Apply one more coat of decoupage glaze and, once dry, add a coat of head cement for a final gloss finish.

SCULPINS & BULLHEADS

It must have been a tie at the beauty contest for fish—and here we have the last place winners. Despite our human prejudice, bottom dwelling sculpins and bullheads (alias catfish, horned pout, stonecat, madtom, and more) represent choice meals for hungry bass, and their imitations belong in every fly fisherman's inventory. Shown on these pages are the standard construction designs; however, it should be emphasized that color can vary widely depending on species, and in combination with the color of the environment in which these fish are found. Generally, they display a certain amount of protective coloration—taking on the color of their surroundings. Most imitations for bass range from 2 to 4 inches long, and are heavily weighted to get them to the bottom. The use of a weed guard is recommended.

SPUDDLER (Dan Bailey's)

Hook:	3X or 4X long, sizes 2 to 10
Thread:	Brown
Tail:	Brown calftail
Body:	Cream wool
Wing	Red squirrel tail over which are 4 grizzly hackles, dyed brown, tied flat on top
Gills:	Red wool
Collar:	Red squirrel tail flared over top half
Head:	Spun & clipped brown antelope body hair

WHIT'S OLIVE MATUKA SCULPIN (Dave Whitlock)

Hook:	Black salmon, sizes 4 to 10
Thread:	Olive
Rib:	Oval gold tinsel
Body:	Olive yarn
Wing:	4 dyed olive grizzly hackles, tied matuka style
Fins:	Prairie chicken or hen mallard breast feathers
Gills:	Red wool wrap in front of body & fins
Head:	Brown, black & olive spun deer body hair

TROTH BULLHEAD (Al Troth)

Hook:	Black salmon, sizes 2 to 8
Thread:	Black
Tail:	White bucktail the length of the body, over which is a longer bunch of black marabou
Body:	White wool
Wing:	Black marabou over which are 10-12 strands of peacock herl, reaching to end of tail, all secured front and rear
Head & Collar:	Dark deer body hair, spun and clipped

TYING THE WOOLHEAD SCULPIN

1. Attach thread at the bend and tie in a piece of medium gold oval tinsel. Also attach a 4 inch length of tan wool or similar body material. If weight is desired, now is the time to wrap a lead wire underbody.

2. Wrap a thick tapered body covering the rear 60 percent of the hook shank. Secure at front and trim away excess.

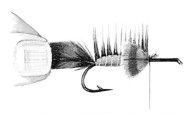

3. Select 2 short body feathers from a hen ringneck pheasant (or similar feathers from a waterfowl breast) and tie in one on each side, concave sides forward, to represent the large fins of a sculpin.

4. Choose 2 or 4 wide, webby brown/grizzly, cree, or similar dyed hackle feathers. Tie on top, in front of the body, so that they extend one body length beyond the bend.

5. With your left hand, pull back on the hackles using the right hand to stroke the fibers to an upright position. Then spiral the tinsel rib forward over the stems, taking care not to bind down individual fibers.

6. Trim away excess tinsel. In front of fins add one turn of bright red wool or dubbing to represent gills. Next spin on 1 bunch of natural brown deer body hair leaving a collar of long natural tips pointing to the rear. Cut the forward butt ends closely and cement.

7. Move the tying thread to the center of the remaining head space. Cut a bunch of tan wool from the skin and slide the bunch over the hook eye keeping the fibers roughly parallel to the hook shank. Three or 4 thread wraps will flare and secure the wool.

8. Repeat with brown wool, then more tan wool to form a mottled effect. Move thread to front of head, tie off, and cement. Remove fly from the vise, and using scissors, trim the wool to the desired shape.

SHAD

Throughout much of the southern United States, in particular the Mississippi River basin and the Gulf Coast states, both the threadfin shad and the gizzard shad are found in abundance, usually in lakes and slow moving rivers. These members of the herring family represent an important food source for black, striped, and white bass. While the gizzard shad can grow to 3 pounds, their young are ideal baitfish during their first year as they grow to 4 to 5 inches, almost the size of a fully mature threadfin shad.

Both species give the fly tyer large size morsels to imitate and three of the best patterns are listed here. All were originated by well known bass fishermen and outstanding fly tyers: Jimmy Nix from Texas designed both the floating and sinking versions of the Shineabou Shad; Oklahoma native Dave Whitlock devised his Prismatic Shad; and another Texan, Al Wilkie, is responsible for the attractive Wilkie's Shad. All of these patterns have been fully described in books and magazines, or on video tape.

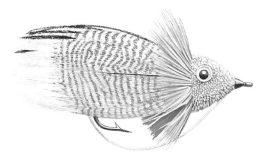

SHINEABOU SHAD

Hook: Mustad 34011, size 4 to 1/0 (3X long, stainless steel)
Underbody: Silver gray Antron dubbing on rear 2/3 of hook shank
Overbody: Fluorescent light gray marabou surrounding the underbody and extending one hook shank length beyond the bend. Add a few strands of silver and pearl Krystal Flash on each side and 6 to 8 peacock herls on top. On each side tie in two mallard flank feathers which extend 1/2" shorter than the marabou
Gills: Dyed red fluff of a saddle hackle, tied on underside
Head: Deer hair dyed gray for topwater shad and gray dyed wool for sinking shad
Eyes: Plastic for floating shad; lead for sinking shad

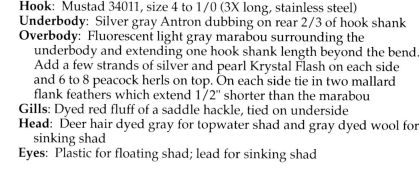

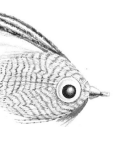

WHITLOCK PRISMATIC SHAD

Hook: 3X to 6X long, nickle plated or stainless steel, sizes 3/0 to 8
Wing: One or two white marabou feathers (including stems) tied in behind the hook eye and extending to beyond the bend
Body: A folded piece of prismatic tape, each side trimmed to the shape shown, and applied from the underside, with the "fold" molding to the hook shank
Topping: 3 to 6 gray ostrich herls, plus three peacock herls
Gills: Red feather fluff
Cheeks: Two gray mallard flank feathers, tied one on each side as shown
Eyes: Doll eyes, or painted yellow with a black pupil

WILKIE'S SHAD

Hook: Single hump popper hook such as Mustad 33900, size 2/0
Body: After wrapping entire rear portion of the hook shank with .030 lead wire, tie in a piece of fine gold wire, then wrap a body of white Sparkle Yarn, winding up to the hump in the hook shank
Wing: Begin by placing one clump of white marabou on top, securing with one turn of the wire as you start the rib winding. Additional marabou clumps are added, each fastened with the wire as the rib moves forward on the hook shank, for a total of 6 bunches. On each side, a sidewing is added of barred teal flank feathers
Gills: A narrow band of red floss wrapped around the wing base
Eyes: Bead chain painted yellow with black pupils
Head: White deer body hair, spun and trimmed as shown

WOOLLY BUGGERS

BLACK-OLIVE WOOLLY BUGGER

PURPLE WOOLLY BUGGER

TWO-TONE WOOLLY BUGGER

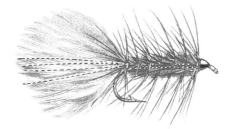

CRYSTAL BUGGER

OLIVE WOOLLY BUGGER

1. Wrap a thread base and tie in a tail of marabou fibers the same length as the hook shank. The optional weight and weedguard may be added at this time.

2. Remove the fuzz from 1/4 inch at the end of a length of chenille and secure the remaining bare threads to the hook. Tie in a saddle hackle by its tip.

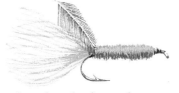

3. Move thread to the front, then wrap chenille forward, secure, and cut off excess chenille.

4. Grasping the saddle hackle by the butt end, spiral it to the front in evenly spaced turns. Secure the hackle, trim excess, whip finish and cement.

It would be hard to deny that the Wooly Bugger has become one of the hottest flies to have evolved in the 1980's. From coast-to-coast this incredibly effective combination of materials has produced bent rods and happy anglers, in search of just about every imaginable gamefish. Not only does it work, it's incredibly simple to tie, and is certainly worthy of a place in every bass fisherman's arsenal.

For many years fly fishermen have appreciated the fish-catching qualities of marabou feathers. In this fly they serve as a tail while many substitutes may be made for the usual chenille body. Also, a wide variety of hooks may be used, although those with a 2X or 3X long shank seem most common. Many fly tyers like to weight this fly with lead wire. Some of the newer synthetic materials can be incorporated into the fly as shown on the Crystal Bugger. Use your imagination and experiment.

POPULAR COMBINATIONS

TAIL	BODY	HACKLE
Black	Black	Black
Brown	Brown	Brown
Black	Peacock	Black
Black	Olive	Black
Olive	Olive	Olive
Purple	Purple	Purple
White	White	White
Yellow	Yellow	Grizzly

zonkers

NATURAL-SILVER ZONKER
Thread: Red
Body: Braided silver mylar tinsel
Fur Strip: Natural gray rabbit
Throat: Yellow hackle

BLACK - GOLD ZONKER
Thread: Black
Body: Braided gold mylar tinsel
Fur Strip: Natural black rabbit
Throat: Orange hackle

WHITE - PEARL ZONKER
Thread: White
Body: Braided pearl mylar tinsel
Fur Strip: White rabbit
Throat: Red hackle

Credit for the invention of the Zonker style fly is generally given to Dan Byford who originally tied his creation for trout. Dan's design worked so well that it quickly received national attention and was modified by both adding a body form, and by adapting it for other gamefish species. The optional base material can range from plastic, to various metals, to epoxy putty, to the floating foams. This variable understructure permits the fly tyer to construct the fly for his particular fishing situation. The original Zonkers had no underbody, and many anglers continue to prefer this style. Shown here are but three of the many color combinations possible.

1. Using size A thread affix a thread base the full length of the shank.

2. Adhesive backed aluminum and lead tapes (or forms) are available which can be folded over the hook shank to create a Zonker body form.

3. Once in place the tape should be trimmed with scissors to the shape indicated.

4. Cut a piece of braided mylar tubing, remove the cotton core, slip over body and tie down at rear. Half hitch, cut thread and repeat at front. Coat entire body with epoxy.

5. Attach and wind 3 to 5 turns of hackle to form a collar and throat.

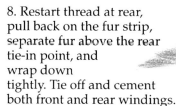

6. Cut a fur strip about 1 1/2 or 2 times the hook shank length, and trim the ends to the shape shown.

7. Securely tie down the front end of the fur strip, build a thread head, whip knot and cut thread.

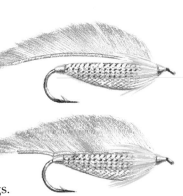

8. Restart thread at rear, pull back on the fur strip, separate fur above the rear tie-in point, and wrap down tightly. Tie off and cement both front and rear windings.

BIBLIOGRAPHY

American Angler & Fly Tyer magazine, various dates North Conway, NH: Northland Press, 1978 - 1988.

Boyle, Robert, and Dave Whitlock, *Fly Tyer's Almanac*. 2nd edition. Piscataway, NJ: Wincheser Press, 1975.

Boyle, Robert and Dave Whitlock, *Second Fly-Tyer's Almanac*. Philadelphia: J.B. Lippincott Co., 1978.

Fly Fisherman magazine, various dates. Harrisburg, PA: Historical Times, 1976 - 1988.

Herter, George L., *Professional Fly Tying and Tackle Making*. 9th edition. Waseca, MN: Herters, Inc. 1953.

Leiser, Eric, *Book of Fly Patterns*. New York: Alfred A. Knopf, 1987.

Leonard, J. Edson, *Flies*. 1950. Reprint. New York: A.S. Barnes & Co. 1953.

Livingston, A.D., *Tying Bugs and Flies for Bass*. Philadelphia: J.B. Lippincott Co., 1977.

Nix, Jimmy, *Tying Bass Flies With Jimmy Nix* (video tape). Jackson Hole, WY: Jack Dennis Video Library, 1988.

Nixon, Tom, *Fly Tying and Fly Fishing for Bass and Panfish*. 2nd edition. New York: A.S. Barnes and Co. 1977.

Stewart, Dick, *The Hook Book*. Intervale, NH: Northland Press, 1986.

Stewart, Dick, *Universal Fly Tying Guide*. North Conway, NH: R.B. Stewart, 1979.

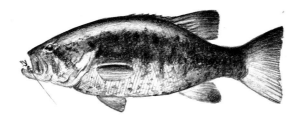

INDEX TO FLY PATTERNS

Alewife	34
Black Bivisible	24
Black-Gold Zonker	46
Black Nosed Dace	34
Black-Olive Woolly Bugger	45
Black Rubberlegs	39
Black Rubbertail	31
Brown Bivisible	24
Cardinelle	18
Clauser's Baby Smallmouth	18
Clauser's Crayfish	20
Crawdad Creeper	20
Crawdad Shedder	20
Crystal Bugger	45
Cupped Popper	40
Dahlberg Diving Bug	22
Dahlberg Diving Minnow	22
Dave's Chamois Leech	33
Dave's Crayfish	21
Dave's Damsel Nymph	39
Dave's Eelworm Streamer	28
Dave's Hopper	29
Drake Nymph	39
Dredgebug	39
Elk Hair Caddis	25
Featherwing Moth	35
Gerbubble Bug	35
Gerbubble Bug (popper)	40
Gray Hairwing Caddis	25
Gray Wulff	24
Hair Moth	35
Henshall Bug	35
Joe's Hopper	29
Lefty's Bug	40
Lefty's Red & White	19
Letort Hopper	29
Li'l Pickerel	19
Marabou Leech	33
Mickey Finn	18

Mizzolian Spook	37
Most Whit Hairbug - Porky's Pet	30
Muddler Minnow	37
Multicolor Marabou Muddler	37
Natural-Silver Zonker	46
Olive Matuka	19
Peacock Devil Bug	25
Pearl Minnow	31
Pencil Popper	40
Purple Wooly Bugger	45
Rabbit Fur Matuka	19
Rabbit Fur Muddler	37
Rabbit Strip Diver	22
Red & White Devil Bug	25
Sang Sinking Frog	27
Schmuecker Bug	31
Shenk's White Streamer	18
Shineabou Shad	44
Skipping Bug	40
Slider	40
Spuddler	42
Swimming Crayfish	21
Swimming Frog	26
Ted's Crayfish	21
The Leech	33
Troth Bullhead	42
Trout Parr	34
Two-Tone Woolly Bugger	45
Ugly Helgy	39
White Marabou Muddler	37
White-Pearl Zonker	46
White Wulff	24
Whitlock Prismatic Shad	44
Whit's Matuka Sculpin	42
Whit's Mouse Rat	36
Wiggle Legs Frog	27
Wilkie's Shad	44
Woolhead Sculpin	43
Yellow Perch	34